around MONTRÉAL with KIDS

by Juliet W

D1161007

1ST EDITION
FODOR'S TRAVEL PUBLICATIONS
New York * Toronto * London * Sydney * Auckland
www.fodors.com

CREDITS
Writer: Juliet Waters

Series Editors: Karen Cure, Andrea Lehman
Editor: Amanda Theunissen
Editorial Production: David Downing
Production/Manufacturing: Angela L. McLean

Design: Fabrizio La Rocca, *creative director*;
Tigist Getachew, *art director*
Cover Art and Design: Jessie Hartland
Flip Art and Illustrations: Rico Lins, Keren Ora
Adomoni/Rico Lins Studio

ABOUT THE WRITER

Juliet Waters was born, raised, and plans to always live in Montréal. She is the book critic for the *Montréal Mirror*, and author of the column "I, Single Mum." She contributes regularly to Canada's top fashion magazine, *Flare*, writes travel articles for *Doctor's Review*, and has written for the *Montréal Gazette* and CBC radio. She lives with her son Ben.

FODOR'S AROUND MONTRÉAL WITH KIDS

First Edition
ISBN 1-4000-1370-4
ISSN 1543-9178

IMPORTANT TIP

Although all prices, opening times, and other details in this book are based on information supplied to us at press time, changes occur all the time in the travel world, and Fodor's cannot accept responsibility for facts that become outdated or for inadvertent errors or omissions. So always confirm information when it matters, especially if you're making a detour to visit a specific place.

SPECIAL SALES

This book is available for special discounts for bulk purchases for sales promotions or premiums. Special editions, including personalized covers, excerpts of existing books, and corporate imprints, can be created in large quantities for special needs. For more information, write to Special Markets/Premium Sales, 1745 Broadway, MD 6-2, New York, New York 10019 or e-mail specialmarkets@randomhouse.com. Inquiries from Canada should be directed to your local Canadian bookseller or sent to Random House of Canada, Ltd., Marketing Department, 2775 Matheson Boulevard East, Mississauga, Ontario L4W 4P7. Inquiries from the United Kingdom should be sent to Fodor's Travel Publications, 20 Vauxhall Bridge Road, London SW1V 2SA, England.

PRINTED IN THE UNITED STATES OF AMERICA
10 9 8 7 6 5 4 3 2 1

COUNTDOWN TO GOOD TIMES

GET READY, GET SET!

Montréal may be one of the oldest cities in North America, but it's a town that loves to try new things. No wonder kids love it! Whether you're visiting for the first time, or have lived here all your life, exploring Montréal with kids is always an adventure. Planning a stress-free outing, however, can be a challenge. That's where this book will help. I've listed 68 of my favorite ways to spend a terrific couple of hours or an entire day with children in tow. I've scoured the city, digging out activities your kids—and you—will love, from a ride on a vintage train at one of North America's largest train museums to a tour of the police cavalry stables in Parc du Mont-Royal. I've added tips on what to watch for and where to eat. So pretty much all you've got to do is grab the book and go!

If you're a tourist in Montréal you're probably going to want to head straight to Old Montréal. My advice is to start with one of the kid-friendly museums like Centre d'Histoire or the Point-à-Callière Museum. Both of these entertaining places give kids a great sense of Montréal's rich history and will make other sight-seeing excursions more interesting. Avoid museum overload by heading to the Old Port district, where you'll find all kinds of outdoor activities. On another day, consider a trip out to the exquisite Montréal Botanical Garden, or the unique and exotic Biodôme. Or just hop the Métro to one of Montréal's megaparks, like Jean-Drapeau or Mont-Royal. Rest assured, with its many excellent parks and historic neighbourhoods, Montréal makes it easy to balance sight-seeing with play. And you'll find Montréal teeming with great places to eat and interesting people to watch. So relax and enjoy your visit.

SAVING MONEY

Only regular adult and kids' prices are listed: children under the ages specified are free. Always ask whether any discounts are offered for a particular status or affiliation (bring your I.D.). Many attractions sell family tickets or long-term memberships. Some places—mostly museums—have free or reduced admission on certain days, or during certain hours. The Montréal Museums pass allows you unlimited visits to most museums over a consecutive two-day period. It can be purchased for $20 at all participating museums. Keep your eye out for the *Passeport POM*, a free booklet packed with discount coupons to most of the major attractions. You can find it at many museums and at any of the INFO-TOURISTE centres (call 514/873–2015 to find the nearest one). Residents of Montréal are eligible for the ACCÈS Montréal card, which gives them discounts and sometimes free admission to certain sites, like the Botanical Garden. Call 514/87–ACCES for information on how to purchase this.

Monthly and weekly (M–Su) Métro passes allow unlimited travel on the Montréal Métro system. Tourist passes good for one or three days are also available at most major Métro stations from April to October, and all year at the Berri-UQAM or Bonaventure stations.

EATING OUT

One of the joys of this city is the abundance of cheap, authentic, often family-run ethnic restaurants. If you're traveling with a picky North American eater, however, don't worry. Few North Americans love the hot dog, fries, and soft drink combo as passionately as French Canadians. There's almost always a neighbourhood snack bar, with the standard kid-friendly menu, somewhere nearby. Montréal also abounds with cafés which serve light, basic meals and great desserts. Some of the better restaurants are closed on Monday, so phone first if that's when you're planning to visit. Most Montréal restaurants have reasonably big no-smoking sections. If second-hand smoke is a concern, make sure to ask for a seat far from the smoking section. All of the outings in this book include tips on where to eat, but if you're looking for more detailed descriptions, *Resto à Go-Go: 180 Cheap and Fun Places to Eat and Drink in Montréal*, by Sarah Musgrave, is Montréal's cheap-eats bible.

GETTING AROUND

Drive defensively in Montréal. The city's drivers are known for their unpredictability. Keep in mind that it is illegal to turn right on a red light here (though this law is slated to change soon). Given that Montréal is world renowned for its clean, quiet, attractive, safe, and inexpensive Métro system, leaving your car at home or at your hotel will save you a lot of stress.

Buses and Métros run according to schedules that are usually posted at stops. A star on the schedule means that the bus is wheelchair-accessible (perfect for strollers). You can also get this information by calling 514/AUTOBUS; or even better, go to the "Azimut" page on the transit commission's Web site (www.stm.info). Type in your departure point (street address, or corner will do), your destination, and estimated time of departure; within seconds you'll be given the three fastest routes, complete with walking distances and the exact time it should take you from your door to wherever you're going.

WHEN TO GO

With the exception of seasonal attractions, kid-oriented destinations are generally busiest when children are out of school—especially on weekends. During the school year some museums may be mobbed with school groups on weekdays. Since these field trips usually finish by early afternoon, after 2 PM can be a good time to visit. The hours listed in this book are the basic hours, not necessarily those applicable on holidays. It's always best to check ahead if you want to see an attraction on a holiday.

RESOURCES AND INFORMATION

The Weekend section of the Saturday *Montréal Gazette* usually has one or two features devoted to family-oriented activities, as well as listings with brief descriptions of special events around town. Tourisme Montréal is an excellent resource for special events and exhibits; call 514/873–2015, or 877/BONJOUR from outside Montréal. Or head directly to the Centre Info-Touriste opposite Dorchester Square (rue Peel, just north of boulevard René-Lévesque). On the Web, Montréal Plus (www.english.montrealplus.ca) has a handy mapping device that locates venues for you.

Prices in this book are listed in Canadian dollars, and according to Canadian usage, words adhere to British spellings (as in "colour"). Take note of the national and local holidays: The Friday before and Monday after Easter; Victoria Day (third Monday in May); Canada Day (July 1); St-Jean Baptiste Day (June 24); Labour Day (first Monday in September); Thanksgiving (second Monday in October); Christmas; Boxing Day (December 26); New Year's Eve; and New Year's Day.

FINAL THOUGHTS
Lots of parents and children were interviewed to create these suggestions, and we'd love to add yours. E-mail us at editors@fodors.com (specify *Around Montréal with Kids* on the subject line), or write to us at Fodor's Around Montréal with Kids, 1745 Broadway, 15th floor, New York, NY 10019.

—Juliet Waters

AQUADÔME

Just because it's snowing, pouring rain, or even just suspiciously cloudy doesn't mean you ever have to miss an exciting, even thrilling, day of water fun. At this awesome indoor water-sports centre, you and your family can speed down a figure-eight waterslide, sit behind a waterfall, crawl along a beach, relax in the Jacuzzi area, or lounge around under a palm tree next to 7.5-metre-high (25-foot-high) picture windows. With the water temperature kept a balmy 30°C (86°F), you might even forget what it's really like outside, even if it's -30°C. In the summer, this is a great place to head if your children are especially sun sensitive, or if you're not sure you can face the pounding sun of a July heat wave.

Most of the action takes place around the leisure pool, a large clover-shaped area, overseen by lifeguards and some pretty creative hanging animal sculptures. Young children can use a slide that sends them into the very, very shallow end. More courageous toddlers can get their head wet by running through the thunderous fountain, then sitting behind the mechanical waterfall area. Flotation boards and noodles fill the pool. Older kids will love

HEY, KIDS! Most people in this neighbourhood are bilingual, so if you're from out of town don't worry about talking to people in English. Here are some French Canadian words and phrases you might hear, or want to try while you're in the pool: *Attention!* (Watch out!); *Attendez!* (Wait!); *Allez!* (Go!); *Arrêt de courir!* (Stop running!); *C'est super fun!;* (This is really fun!); *Il est super cute!* (He's really cute!).

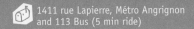 1411 rue Lapierre, Métro Angrignon
and 113 Bus (5 min ride)

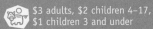 $3 adults, $2 children 4–17,
$1 children 3 and under

 M and W–F 9–4, Tu 9–1:30,
Sa–Su 12–8

 514/367–6460

 All ages

the three giant waterslides—the 60-metre (197-foot) figure eight, and two steep enclosed slides.

For the serious swimmers there's an Olympic-sized pool, which is usually sectioned off into two 25-metre pools, a shallow one and a deep one. Here, there's another slide and diving boards. Large groups can take advantage of volleyball, basketball, and water-polo equipment. Aquadôme also offers courses in sports such as synchronized swimming and underwater hockey.

There are three changing rooms, including a unisex family room with a diaper-changing area and blow dryers. About the only down side of Aquadôme is that on a busy weekend it can get pretty noisy. If your kids are old enough to leave unsupervised, you can always take a break in the snack bar that overlooks the leisure pool.

EATS FOR KIDS
The snack bar has a good selection ranging from sandwiches to hot dogs. There's also a nearby **Pizza Hut** (7551 blvd. Newman, 514/595–7474), and a **Chez Cora** (7573 blvd. Newman, 514/364–5884), a popular brunch chain. Nearby Angrignon Park is an excellent place to picnic.

KEEP IN MIND Children 7 and under must be accompanied by an adult. An adult must be in the water with children aged 5 or under. Children must be at least 120 centimetres (48 inches) tall to use the big slide. The slide is only open during set hours according to a rather complicated schedule, so if you have older kids, call ahead to make sure it will be open when you go. The pool is reserved for swimming lessons on weekend mornings.

67

With the sun pouring down through the glass ceiling, this warm little patch of ice is the perfect place to introduce your kids to the joys of skating. It's also the classiest indoor rink in the city. On a hot summer day you can skate around in shorts, making it a fun alternative to the pool. In the winter you can enjoy the feeling of open sky without having to worry about mittens and scarves. And since it's right downtown you can combine a little skating with tons of other activities.

Saturday mornings are the optimal time to flounder around the rink with novice skaters. There's child-friendly music, and the hour between 10:30 and 11:30, designated tiny-tot time, is reserved for kids under 12. If you can't make it on a Saturday, just about any weekday is also safe for young kids to learn (Sunday can be too crowded); the rink is pretty small, so stronger skaters can't build up enough speed to cause dangerous collisions. Whenever

EATS FOR KIDS The rink is surrounded by a very comfortable, surprisingly elegant food court. **Eurosnacks** has a great selection of grilled sandwiches. If you're looking for something healthy try **Veggirama,** or if you just want a good cup of coffee or cocoa head to **Café Suprême.**

HEY, KIDS! A New Yorker named Jackson Haines is considered the father of figure skating. In 1863 and '64 he won the Championships of America. His fellow Americans, however, were uncomfortable with the freedom and expression he brought to the sport. He ended up moving to Europe where he was much more popular. A Montrealer, Louis Rubinstein, is considered to be the first person who thought of organizing skating as an international sport. He laid the groundwork for uniform competitions and testing. If it wasn't for these two men, world-class figure-skating competition wouldn't exist today.

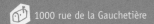 1000 rue de la Gauchetière

 $5.50 adults, $3.50 children 16 and under; $4.50 skate rental

 Su-Th 11:30–9, F 11:30 AM–12 AM, Sa 10:30 AM–12 AM

 514/395-0555, www.le1000.com

 2 and up

you go, you can rent skates and helmets on-site, there are metal walkers for kids to help them with balance, and there are railings all the way around the rink—especially useful if you're not a strong skater yourself. If you haven't taken out your own skates for a while, there's on-site skate sharpening. The Atrium is also a great place for a birthday party. Packages for 12 people or more include a cake, helmets, balloons, and a visit from the rink's friendly mascot, Émile. You can make your birthday party reservations online at www.le1000.com.

If you have young teenagers they might be interested in Friday disco night, which starts at 7 PM and is open to kids 13 and up. Of course they'll probably hint that you should go hide in the adjacent food court, or better yet, leave; but with all the stuff to do nearby, you might not mind giving them a little space for a while.

KEEP IN MIND This is an ideal summer skating rink. In the winter, of course, you have a lot more options to choose from. There are 168 skating rinks in and around Montréal. The most popular outdoor ones are Beaver Lake (see #66), Parc Lafontaine, and the Bonsecours Basin (see #21). If you want to avoid the crowds, your best bet is the Olympic Rowing Basin on Île Notre-Dame (see #19), or the frozen lake at Jarry Park (see #43).

BEAVER LAKE

Before you go, make sure your kids are not expecting to find beavers here. Beavers did once live in the swamp this man-made lake was created from, but they took off into the woods long ago. Even without those little buck-toothed creatures, however, your kids will find plenty to enjoy on the western slope of Parc du Mont-Royal. If they keep their eyes peeled they may spot the odd muskrat, and there is always a nice big family of ducks living on the lake.

Summer here is heaven for young children. If you call ahead and reserve, a 20-minute tour of the police cavalry stables (1515 chemin Camillien-Houde, 514/280–2777) is a particular thrill. If you don't have a reservation, you can always visit the horses in the pen outside, and don't hesitate to approach mounted police to pet their noble, well-behaved steeds. You can also rent paddleboats ($8 for 30 minutes) to cruise the lake, or head to the great playground, located along the path, southwest of the Chalet. The highlight of the day, however, may be the long grassy hill that offers endless possibilities for running and tumbling.

GETTING THERE If you're driving, head up chemin Remembrance, just off Côte-des-Neiges, and you'll find plenty of parking right next to the park. You can also take the 11 Bus from Métro Mont-Royal, which stops in front of the cavalry stables. Or, you can take the 165 Bus from Métro Guy. This will drop you off at the Trafalgar Stairs on Côtes-des-Neiges. If you're walking up from Jeanne Mance Park, or rue Peel, take the stairs that continue up from the rue Peel entrance (see #20). They're a physical challenge, but they'll save you about 30 minutes of walking.

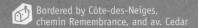 Bordered by Côte-des-Neiges, chemin Remembrance, and av. Cedar

 Free

 Park daily 6 AM–11 PM; Chalet daily 10–8

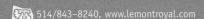 514/843-8240, www.lemontroyal.com

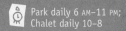 All ages

Older kids might be interested in peering through or climbing on the funky sculptures near Maison Smith, a pretty stone house with an exhibit on the history of Parc du Mont-Royal. These sculptures are often used as goalposts in games of Frisbee soccer. Young teenagers will love the beachlike atmosphere along the slope on sunny days.

Winter, however, is really the best season for older kids. They'll get a huge thrill from the ice slides built to accommodate inner tubes. The lake freezes over for skating and kids who are new to cross-country skiing can get some great practice. The park also has one of the best tobogganing hills in the city. If you don't have your own equipment, don't worry; skates, skis, and tubes are all available for rent at the Chalet.

EATS FOR KIDS

This is an excellent picnic park, though you can get a simple lunch at the Chalet next to the lake. There's another chalet at the lookout point (see Olmsted Road). If it's not winter, it's worth the 10-minute walk to get there; the food is the same, but the view is spectacular.

HEY, KIDS! Don't make the mistake of thinking that the police here are Mounties just because they're on horses. The Royal Canadian Mounted Police (RCMP) are Canada's federal police, kind of like the American FBI. They were created back in the 19th century when Canadians were settling Western Canada. It was pretty wild back then, so horses were essential. The police in Parc du Mont-Royal are city police, and they're on horseback for a reason. There's not much crime here, but when it does happen it's usually on the steep wooded trails. Horseback is really the best and only way to patrol this area.

BIODÔME

65

Can't bear another sweltering July afternoon? Head to the Arctic and watch penguins rocket through the water. What to do on a freezing Sunday in January? Go on a walking safari through an Amazonian forest. See if you can spot the endangered golden lion tamarin monkey, a sloth hanging from a tree, or a capybara, the world's largest rodent. After little more than a decade of growth, the Biodôme continues to get more interesting every year as its four re-created indoor ecosystems mature. The leaves and flowers even change with the seasons, just as they would in their natural environments, and the animals hibernate in the same way they would in their native habitats.

In the tropical forest your children can spot reptilian caimans camouflaged in the mud, a yellow anaconda snake, and the hyacinth macaw (the world's largest species of parrot). They can visit a bat cave, and a deceptively beautiful collection of poison frogs (safely kept behind Plexiglas). Make sure you save a chunk of time for the Laurentian Forest,

EATS FOR KIDS You can get a full meal in **La Brise** cafeteria, or a muffin or salad at **Le Nordet** snack bar. If you're going to the Botanical Garden (*see #29*), there are some nice restaurants and a cafeteria there. You can also picnic at nearby Maisonneuve Park.

HEY, KIDS! Have you heard bad things about bats? Think again! Bats have an unfair reputation. They may look like mice with wings, but bats are an entirely different species. They rarely carry disease, they don't nest, they only breed once a year, and they don't bite. You really have to be mean to a bat to make it aggressive. Bats use sonar to detect nearby objects, kind of like whales or dolphins. So if you ever end up in a room with a bat, don't be afraid; try and think of it as a flying dolphin.

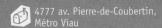 4777 av. Pierre-de-Coubertin, Métro Viau

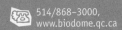 514/868-3000, www.biodome.qc.ca

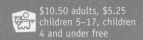 $10.50 adults, $5.25 children 5–17, children 4 and under free

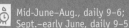 Mid-June–Aug., daily 9–6; Sept.–early June, daily 9–5

 All ages

with its showy otters, shy beavers, and regal lynx. In the St. Lawrence Marine Ecosystem kids can sit and watch schools of giant cod shift with the current, and even spot a shark. The Polar World may not have the same variety of animals, but when the penguins are in the right mood you'll have a hard time tearing your family away.

Remember to remind kids that animals like to nap and have a lot of personal time. Children will need to be patient and willing to backtrack if they want to spot some of their favorites. If the otters are napping, it's definitely worth waiting for them to wake up.

If you're bringing a toddler, don't expect to cover everything. Though there's much to fascinate them here, it can be a little overwhelming. Your own little wild animal may suddenly become obsessed with sliding down the wheelchair ramp as a hint that he's ready for *his* personal time.

KEEP IN MIND There are some interesting exhibit rooms in the Biodôme, but if you're only in Montréal for a short time, it's worth skipping these and heading over to the incredible Botanical Garden (see #29). If that's your plan, expect this to be a fascinating but long day because there's a lot to see. Save some walking time by taking the free shuttle bus from the Biodôme to the Botanical Garden entrance near the Insectarium (see #44). There are picnic tables and a playground there if you want to take a break.

BIOSPHÈRE

Even if your kids aren't immediately curious about the only museum of water in North America, they'll be impressed by the size and originality of this spherical building. The striking geodesic dome was originally the American Pavilion in Expo '67. Though much of the educational material will be too sophisticated for very young children, they'll enjoy tagging along, and you may have a hard time dragging them out of the toddler-sized wooden ship in the lobby.

Fortunately, the current exhibits live up to their inspiring setting. The darkened Discovery Room is full of dramatic lighting and riveting facts about global warming and the impact of melting icebergs on water levels. A giant globe in the centre shows global currents with blinking red and green lights. Interactive-computer terminals educate kids about the impact of changing water levels on their lives, and the lives of plants and animals. A creative workshop area changes from year to year but always centres around a theme like water

HEY, KIDS! The Biosphère was designed in 1967 by the famous American architect Richard Buckminster Fuller. Even back then he believed that we had to stop wasting the Earth's natural resources. He considered the triangle the perfect form, and built this geodesic dome entirely of triangles. Because of the way triangles support each other, this dome uses one-fiftieth of the materials used in a conventional architectural design. Unfortunately, geodesic domes require massive ventilation and fire-prevention systems. In 1976 the acrylic covering he designed was destroyed by fire in half an hour. Still, the structure was miraculously undamaged.

160 Chemin Tour-de-l'Île, near Métro Parc Jean-Drapeau

514/283-5000, www.biosphere.ec.gc.ca

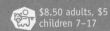$8.50 adults, $5 children 7–17

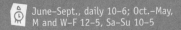June–Sept., daily 10–6; Oct.–May, M and W–F 12–5, Sa–Su 10–5

7 and up

bugs or water fountains. In the Water Delights exhibit, water is examined in myth, religion, and leisure. This section is fun for young children because there are weird whale sounds, re-creations of vacation areas, and a Greek foot bath; but educationally it's a bit unfocused.

Take the elevator up to the Visions exhibit on the fifth floor. A tour guide gives an interesting and, frankly, disturbing lecture on how increasingly sinking water levels in the St. Lawrence River will eventually damage our way of life. The last stop is a trip out to the deck which offers a stunning view of the Lachine Canal. This is where your older children may start asking some difficult questions, such as: isn't the Lachine Canal, and the industrialization it facilitated, a big part of the problem? To answer that you can always propose doing a little field research together (see #37 and #38). Have fun finding the answers.

EATS FOR KIDS

There's a cafeteria here with a great view. You can also picnic in Parc Jean-Drapeau (see #19), grab something at one of the snack bars, or wait to eat at a nearby attraction like La Ronde (see #10), the Stewart Museum (see #5), or the beach on Île Notre-Dame (see #14).

GETTING THERE You can drive here, but somehow it's more fun to take the Métro. Remember to point out to kids that the Métro actually goes underneath the Lachine Canal. There's also an excellent bike path that goes over Pont de la Concorde. You can rent bikes in the Old Port (see #21) and then bike over the bridge to the Biosphère. After your visit, you can bike around the island, or around the Grand Prix circuit (see #19). Think of the natural resources you'll be conserving!

CANADIAN CENTRE FOR ARCHITECTURE

Here's your kid's chance to build a modern-day castle inside a modern-day castle. At least one Sunday, and sometimes two, a month, the Canadian Centre for Architecture (CCA) takes out some of its 150 building sets for family workshops. Kids get the chance to play with some of the best, newest, and coolest building blocks and construction sets on the market, and they get to do it in the most luxurious play space in the city. Though there are themes like Around the World in 20 Toys or Ingenious Architecture, these are free-form workshops without instruction. Toys are simply put out on tables for kids to do what they want with for 90 minutes.

Little brains will be so focused on building an ancient temple, a middle-eastern mosque, or a wild west trading post that they probably won't notice the incredible room that surrounds them. Parents, however, will appreciate the exquisite detail, the grooved columns, and

EATS FOR KIDS Up the street is an exceptional food emporium, **Le Faubourg Ste-Catherine** (1616 rue Ste-Catherine Ouest, 514/939–3663). If the weather is nice, try **Pagnelli's Bakery** on the ground floor, which has a pretty terrace out back.

HEY, KIDS! When you think building sets, you probable think Lego. The Lego company was started by Ole Kirk Christiansen, a carpenter who used to make small models of his products. The name Lego comes from the Danish phrase *leg godt*, which means play well. The company started making toys from plastic after World War II. Its first automatic-binding bricks were produced in 1949. Over the years, wheels, gears, and motors were added. In 1966 Lego produced the first train equipped with rails and a 4.5-volt motor.

Su workshops 11 AM, 1:30 PM, 3 PM

 1920 rue Baile, Métro Guy

514/939-7026,
www.cca.qc.ca

Family workshop $4 adults,
$2 children 10 and under

3-10

the marble mantelpiece. Though most parents prefer to spend the time building with their kids, you'll sometimes find a few congregating in the opulent adjacent sunroom. The labor of love of Bronfman family heiress Phyllis Lambert, the CCA is one of the foremost museums of architecture in the world and it certainly looks the part. No expense seems to have been spared in building this museum and restoring the two Golden Square Mile mansions that have been incorporated into it.

This is the perfect Sunday activity for budding architects, urban planners, and real-estate moguls. A bonus for parents is that someone else puts the blocks away, and there are no little pieces to step on, ever. Reservations are essential, and it's best to book a couple of weeks ahead. These workshops are so popular that kids have been known to call up and reserve themselves.

KEEP IN MIND If you only see the CCA from rue Baile, it will probably remind you of a prison. For a more impressive view, walk around to boulevard René-Lévesque and you'll see the two gorgeous houses, known collectively as Shaugnessy House, that have been incorporated into the museum. On the other side of boulevard René-Lévesque, you can visit the CCA gardens where you'll find an eccentric collection of sculptures overlooking the Décarie Expressway.

CAP-SAINT-JACQUES

One of the great things Montréal has going for families is the number of nature parks on the outskirts of the city. Of all of them, Cap-Saint-Jacques reigns supreme in size and in the range of things to do. Hike, bike, hang out on pretty little stretches of beach, or hunt for turtles along the shoreline. Canoe, kayak, or spend the day learning about organic farming on an actual working farm. All of these things can be done at a sanctuary only 30 minutes from downtown.

The beach is the biggest draw in the summer, and like the public pools, is open for swimming as soon as school holidays start. Located on the Lake of Two Mountains, it is clean and scenic. It can, however, get pretty crowded on weekends and really hot days. Flee the crowds by renting a canoe, kayak, or pedal boat and drifting along the shoreline. If you've brought bikes, or in-line skates, you can take advantage of the 7-km (4-mi) bike path. Or, you can hike the 17 km (10 mi) of trails.

HEY, KIDS! So what is organic farming? To understand that question you have to know that farmers have lots of challenges, and their biggest challenge is bugs. Some bugs eat plants and stop them from growing, others eat the fruits and vegetables we want. Most farmers use chemicals to kill bugs, but some worry that those chemicals aren't very healthy for humans. Organic farming tries to solve this problem by finding ways to use less chemicals. For example, they sometimes use bugs to eat other bugs. Lady bugs don't eat plants, but one lady bug can eat up to 5,000 other bugs!

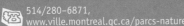 20 099 blvd. Gouin Ouest

 $4 per car; beach fees
$4 adults, $3 children 6–13

Beach mid-June–Aug., 10–7;
farm daily sunrise–sunset

514/280–6871,
www.ville.montreal.qc.ca/parcs-nature

All ages

For young children an afternoon at the organic farm is sheer bliss. Though this farm does actually produce and sell vegetables, it's mainly designed to entertain kids. One field is home to an array of supermodel cows and bulls, the golden long-haired breed you usually only see in cheese ads. The barn is full of squeaky clean pigs, goats, sheep, and horses; and the farmyard is busy with chickens, ducks, and bunnies. Ostriches race each other in an adjacent field. There are puppet shows, farm tours, and, for a few extra dollars, horse-and-cart and donkey rides.

The farm is open year-round and is also a popular spot for winter sugaring-off parties. If you're bringing a toddler, bring a change of clothes. Little farm fans have been known to throw themselves screaming into the closest mud puddle upon learning there are no plans to move here permanently.

EATS FOR KIDS
There's plenty of picnic space here. A restaurant in an old stone house near the beach serves fast food. The food and snack bar at the farm restaurant has a bit more variety, and there are seasonal treats at the General Store.

GETTING THERE If you're driving, take Highway 40 to Exit 49 for rue Ste-Marie, and follow the PARC NATURE signs. From Highway 20, take rue St-Charles north to boulevard Gouin and turn left. If you don't have a car, you can take the 68 Bus, from Métro Henri-Bourassa, or Métro Côte-Vertu, which stops at the entrance and at a second stop 1 km from the beach. Keep in mind that this can take almost two hours from downtown.

CENTAUR THEATRE

Yes, there is an alternative to Saturday morning cartoons. The Petro-Canada Saturday Morning Children's Theatre Series is a great way to introduce kids to live performance. The beautiful Centaur Theatre, situated in the Old Stock Exchange building in Old Montréal, adds some elegance to this outing. While it's always tempting to cocoon on frigid fall and winter mornings when the theatre season is in full swing, once you're in the presence of laughing children and energetic actors you'll know it's worth the effort.

These productions are staged at least one Saturday a month and are generally aimed at school-age children. Sophistication varies, however, so check the Centaur's program beforehand. This is one of those outings where attention to age range is truly essential, since a bored child can ruin a show for other kids. A play like *Night Light*, about a young child and a scaly one-eyed monster named Tara, would be fine for preschoolers. Other

EATS FOR KIDS For a fun after-theatre lunch, **Casa de Mateo** (440 rue St-Francois Xavier, 514/844–7448) is a festive family-style Mexican restaurant. If you're looking for a light, but exceptional early brunch, head to **Olive et Gourmando** (*see* Pointe-à-Callière Museum).

KEEP IN MIND Children's theatre in Montréal is almost always in either English or French. The far better-subsidized French theatre scene is often where you'll find the most exciting productions. If your child is bilingual, La Maison Theatre (245 rue Ontario Est, 514/288–7211, www.maisontheatre.qc.ca) is dedicated solely to children's theatre. Some of the productions designed for preschoolers rely heavily on puppets, set design, and physical comedy, so even children with little understanding of French will probably still enjoy going. And what better way to get them interested in learning a new language!

 453 rue St-Francois Xavier

 514/288–3161,
www.centaurtheatre.com

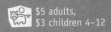 $5 adults,
$3 children 4–12

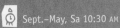 Sept.–May, Sa 10:30 AM

 4 and up

shows like *The Dragon's Heart*, about a young princess who surfs the Internet and meets a black dragon who asks too many questions, would be better for older children. If you're unsure, call the box office for suggested age range. Reservations are always a good idea, and essential around Christmas.

The Centaur is far from the only place in Montréal to find excellent children's theatre. There are children's theatre companies staging plays all over town. Geordie Productions is one of the most active companies. Visit their Web site at www.geordie.ca, or call 514/845–9810 to find out where and when they're performing. Another place to check out is the Saidye Bronfman Centre for the Arts (5170 chemin de la Côte Ste-Catherine, 514/739–2301). In January and February, they host Artapalooza, a children's theatre festival where companies from around the world arrive to stage three weeks of productions.

HEY, KIDS! One of the most famous child-theatre actors in recent history is Andrea McArdle, who had the lead role in the original Broadway production of *Annie* when she was only 12. As an adult actor, she's not exactly a household name, mostly because she never pursued a career in TV or movies, but she's still famous on Broadway. Not long ago she was the star of the Broadway production *Beauty and the Beast*. At the same time her daughter, Alexis Kalehoff, had an important role in another big Broadway production down the street, *Les Misérables*. Alexis was only 10!

CENTRE D'HISTOIRE DE MONTRÉAL

Your first question upon entering this colourful, dynamic museum will probably be: What are those sirens? That's the sound of the Canadian Parliament building being burnt to the ground by angry mobs in 1849. How perfect that this museum, devoted to Montréal's history, is housed in an early-20th-century fire station, right across the street from where the old parliament building once stood.

You won't have to spend much time here before you realise this is not your average history museum. Kids will be easily drawn into a journey through three centuries thanks to dramatically narrated anecdotes from history. Visitors listen to these stories inside bilingual audio chambers, that are a little like phone booths, placed throughout the exhibit. It helps, of course, that Montréal's history is full of conflict: from the battles between Native Americans and settlers in the 17th century; to the Colonial wars of the 18th century; to the riots over language, religion, and working conditions in the 19th century; to the terrorist bombing

HEY, KIDS! Look for a picture of children watching the army march through the streets of Montréal in October, 1970. The army was sent in when the Front de la Libération du Québec (FLQ) kidnapped a government minister. These terrorists wanted Québec to be its own country. They were caught, but only after the minister was murdered. That was the end of the FLQ, but many people still wanted Québec to be separate from Canada. In 1995 there was a vote and the separatists lost by only a tiny margin. Québec is still part of Canada now, but you never know!

335 Place d'Youville,
Métro Square Victoria

514/872-3207,
www2.ville.montreal.qc.ca

$4.50 adults,
$3 kids 6–17

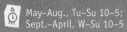
May–Aug., Tu–Su 10–5;
Sept.–April, W–Su 10–5

6 and up

and separatism of the 20th century. Fortunately, Montréal has not only survived all this conflict, but thrived. As evidence, kids will find inspiring stories of social harmony: from a massive funeral procession for a highly respected native chief in the 18th century to Expo '67, the most exciting world's fair of the 20th century. As a journalist in *Harper's New Monthly Magazine* wrote in 1889, "Montréal is a striking exception to the text that a house divided against itself cannot stand," a statement that seems to be as true as it ever was.

Like most museums in Old Montréal, Centre d'Histoire offers a great view of the Old Port. A rooftop stroll takes you from the permanent to the temporary exhibit. Don't miss it, even if you aren't staying for the second exhibit. After learning about Montréal's past, it's always fun to get a bird's-eye view of its present.

EATS FOR KIDS

If you're visiting during the week, try **Titanic** (445 rue St-Pierre, 514/849–0894). This funky luncheonette is sunken below street level and has great sandwiches. It can get pretty crowded at noon, so it's best to go in the early afternoon.

KEEP IN MIND Some adults have complained that the exhibit is confusing and doesn't provide enough context for tourists. This is probably less of a problem for kids who are more interested in history's stories than in dry introductory narrative. If you want more context, however, you might want to consider a visit to the McCord Museum of Canadian History (*see #31*), or the nearby Pointe-à-Callière Museum (*see #12*). Centre d'Histoire also offers some great walking tours of Old Montréal, but they're usually in French. For English walking tours try Guidatour (514/844–4021).

CÉRAMIC CAFÉ STUDIO

Looking for the perfect gift for a much-loved teacher or grandparent? Or, if you're visiting, maybe your child would like a unique souvenir, something other than a T-shirt? Instead of spending hours shopping, consider hanging out together, nibbling on a pastry, and personalizing a piece of pottery. Your child will end up with a professionally glazed coffee mug, flower vase, or dog-food bowl, not to mention that special feeling of accomplishment you get from making something beautiful.

It's a perfect scenario, but it'll cost you. Add up the hourly rate, the price of the unfinished pottery, the latte, the juice, a few treats, and a tip for the waitress/instructor who may have one hell of a cleanup job, and that pretty coffee mug could set you back at least $30. Tack on another $5 if you want the piece ready in under a week. At least Céramic Café Studio makes it virtually impossible to end up with a lame piece, so you will get

KEEP IN MIND The chance to stroll down rue St-Denis and hang out in nearby Carré St-Louis (see #13) is part of the fun of this outing, but if the West End of the city is more convenient for you, **Café Art Folie** (6127 av. Monkland, 514/487–6066) is very similar and more reliably bilingual.

HEY, KIDS! To make sure your pieces turn out the way you like, keep these helpful tips in mind: Start with the palest colours first, and make sure you give each coat about 5 minutes to dry. You should probably paint two coats of each colour to get the best results. If you're using a stencil, you may want to retrace the figure with a thin line of black after you're done painting to make it look really cool. There's a special plastic container with black paint just for this technique.

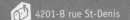 4201-B rue St-Denis

 514/848-1119

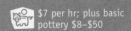 $7 per hr; plus basic pottery $8–$50

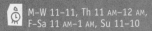 M–W 11–11, Th 11 AM–12 AM, F–Sa 11 AM–1 AM, Su 11–10

 7 and up

your money's worth. The shelves are full of excellent examples of designs that appeal to both children and adults. If your family isn't especially creative, there are stencils of animals, quirky figures, and designs that all look like you drew them off the top of your head. The carbon from the stencil comes off during the glazing process. All you have to do is paint inside the lines.

This is an especially great outing for mothers and daughters—and an especially bad outing for young children. In a good mood they'll be attracted by all the quirky, shiny, brightly coloured animal pottery and want to handle them like toys. In a bad mood they'll be destroying the atmosphere of relaxed concentration. It would be best to save this outing until your kids are old enough to understand the quiet discipline necessary for a great masterpiece.

EATS FOR KIDS **Céramic Café Studio** has a nice selection of pastries and cookies. If you're looking for more of a meal, walk south on rue St-Denis and then west along avenue Duluth and try **Chez José** (*see* Plateau Mont-Royal) for great Mexican food. If you want to save a bit of money walk east on rue Rachel and picnic at beautiful Parc Lafontaine (*see* Maison des Cyclists).

CHÂTEAU RAMEZAY MUSEUM

Few adults, let alone kids, know that Montréal was briefly an American city between 1775 and 1776. Château Ramezay was the headquarters of the American Revolutionaries who invaded and briefly captured the city. This is one of the many interesting historical facts you'll discover in this splendid 300-year-old stone house that is teeming with wonderful artifacts from Montréal's earliest years.

Even before you reach the room devoted to the American occupation, there's much to fire kids' imaginations. In the first room they'll see wonderful little 17th-century postcard etchings of settlers meeting native people; a cradle board used to keep infants snug and mobile; tiny snowshoes; whalebone Inuit snow goggles; beaver pelts from the fur trade; a shaman rattle; and the cross stick carried by the fierce, devoted Catholic missionaries or *Sorciers de Dieu* (God's Sorcerers). As you progress through the first few rooms, kids will learn about how the native peoples participated in the battles between the French and British until

HEY, KIDS! American Revolutionaries arrived on the Island of Montréal on Sunday, November 12, 1775. Knowing the usual weather in mid-November, most Montrealers wouldn't recommend a visit, let alone an invasion! The Americans were in trouble from the start. In 1776 Benjamin Franklin arrived to help. He brought a printer, Fleury Mesplet, to establish a newspaper to convince Montrealers to rebel against the British. But Montrealers had a hard time believing that this occupying army was really here to liberate them. After 188 days the Americans retreated. Mesplet, however, stayed behind and founded the city's first newspaper, the *Montréal Gazette*.

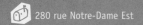 280 rue Notre-Dame Est

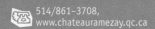 514/861-3708,
www.chateauramezay.qc.ca

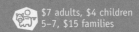 $7 adults, $4 children
5–7, $15 families

 June–Sept., daily 10–6;
Oct.–May, Tu–Su 10–4:30

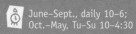 5 and up

the French surrendered New France in 1763. After learning more about the ill-fated American invasion, they'll learn how Montréal developed under British colonization. They'll see model ships and trains from Montréal's industrialization period, some of Montréal's first bicycles, and even the first car, sporting Montréal's first license plate.

Much of the basement has been restored to illustrate daily life during the early centuries. A tiny double-deckered children's bed from 1845 poignantly illustrates how much smaller the average 19th-century child was. There are looms, ovens, and examples of the casual indoor clothes Montréal's upper classes would have worn. In the last room don't miss the 17th-century dog-powered roasting spit. Some families used dogs in small wooden cages, a little like hamster wheels, to keep their roasts turning.

EATS FOR KIDS
The museum café is managed by Claude Postel (see Notre-Dame Basilica), famous for its pastries. If you prefer to visit Place Jacques-Cartier, try **Le Jardin Nelson** (407 Place Jacques-Cartier, 514/861–5731), which has a great terrace and light meals from crêpes to pasta.

KEEP IN MIND Even if you don't visit the museum, you can still take a stroll in the Governor's Garden. It's a lovely retreat from the grey cobblestone streets of Old Montréal. Though it's not an exact replica of the garden that once stretched all the way down to the Old Port, it's true to the gardens of the upper classes of New France. There are three sections: the kitchen garden, the flower garden, and an orchard. All are bordered by a medicinal garden. During the summer the museum features guided tours, traditional music, soap making, and similar demonstrations.

COSMODÔME

Your kids may never grow up to work on a spaceship, but that doesn't mean they can't benefit from some astronaut training. It's hard to think of a better way to get kids interested in science and technology. How good is Canada's only Space Camp? Alan B. Shephard, the first American launched into space, who had visited every Space Camp in the world, declared this one "by far the best" at its inauguration in 1994.

Before you enroll, however, you might want to try the drop-in, self-guided visit to the Cosmodôme's Science Centre. Start with the 20-minute multimedia presentation in the Time and Space Machine, a moving platform under a 360-degree screen, which takes you on a trip through the history of space travel. Next, the Telecommunications room teaches about satellite technology through experiments that will let your family hear each other whisper with 45 feet between you. You'll learn about rocket technology in the Conquest of Space room with the benefit of close to 20 interactive terminals. In rooms devoted to moon exploration and the solar system, kids will find pieces of

EATS FOR KIDS If the astronaut food packs at the gift shop (strawberry, ice-cream sandwich, and Neapolitan flavors) aren't enough to curb your appetite, you should be able to find something at **Graffiti's** (2055 Autoroute des Laurentides, 450/686–7696), known for their pasta buffet and fresh foccacia bread.

HEY, KIDS! Space Camp was the brainchild of Dr. Werner Von Braun, who designed the *Saturn V* rocket, which you'll learn about at the Cosmodôme. His dream was that the U.S. space program could be used to get kids interested in science and tap their huge potential to make the world a better place. The first Space Camp was opened in Huntsville, Alabama, in 1982. It was such a big hit that there are now three in the U.S., one in Belgium, one in Japan, and this one in Canada.

 2150 Autoroute des Laurentides (Hwy. 15)

450/978-3615 Science Centre,
800/565-2267 Space Camp,
www.cosmodome.org

 $10 adults, $6.50
children 6-18

 Mid-June–Aug., daily 10–6;
Sept.–early June, Tu–Su 10–6

Science Centre 6 and up;
Space Camp 9 and up

moon rock and a full astronaut uniform. They can even find out what they weigh on each of the planets.

If your child is at least 9 years old you can call to reserve a "Gemini," or half-day visit, to the Space Camp. This gives kids a chance to visit an exact-scale model of the space shuttle *Endeavour*. Space Camp recruits are trained in this model, and get to go on a simulated mission. Visitors also get to see demonstrations of the NASA simulators used to create the feeling of weightlessness and disorientation, and even try some of them out. They'll learn about things like rocket propulsion and how astronauts work in zero-gravity conditions, and they'll get to fool around with all kinds of interactive stations. At this point your kids may be satisfied with everything they've learned. It's more likely, however, that they'll start working on you to enroll them in the weekend or week-long Space Camp adventure. In the future, maybe there will be a special parent camp with advanced training that simulates this exact situation.

KEEP IN MIND If you're interested in an extended stay at Space Camp there are two options. The MIR weekend allows parents to accompany children for three days and two nights. This gives you and your kids the chance to test drive some of the simulators, participate in a mission simulation on the *Endeavour* and at mission control, and participate in various workshops. The ALPHA week is reserved for kids 9–14. They get to test all the simulators, help construct a rocket, sleep for a night on the *Endeavour*, and eat astronaut food.

ÉCOLE DE CIRQUE DE VERDUN

If you live in Montréal, one thing you never have to worry about is your child running away to join the circus. Montréal is home base and farm camp for the world-renowned Cirque du Soleil. Most of their performers are trained at Montréal's École Nationale de Cirque, which offers a professional degree in circus arts. For aspiring young performers École de Cirque de Verdun offers its own introduction to the circus world.

Inside this bright yellow, blue, and red arena you'll find kids of all ages juggling, balancing, swinging, tumbling, bouncing on the trampoline, and hanging from aerial equipment. Every year about 15,000 kids pass through this arena as students, part of school groups, or in summer day camps. The most talented students work on a show that is given annually at the Montréal Jazz Festival. The school also has several open houses throughout the year and puts together initiation workshops that are offered throughout the city, the most popular on Canada Day (July 1) at the Old Port.

HEY, KIDS! Cirque du Soleil was formed in 1984 by a troupe of street performers known as *Le Club des Talons Hauts* (the high-heels club). Back then only 73 people worked for the Cirque. Today there are 2,500 employees worldwide, and in 2003 they put on nine different shows that were watched by about 7 million people. Most of the kids that train at École de Cirque de Verdun won't go on to be performers, but they might become technicians or get one of the many other jobs at the circus. One thing is for sure, they will all become expert fans.

 5190 blvd. LaSalle

 Free to visit; $125–$315 for
14-week course, depending on level

Daily, schedule varies

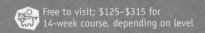 514/768-5812

3 and up

If your child wants to try out some activities before enrolling for a course you'll have to call to find out about open houses or workshops. (If they absolutely must swing on a trapeze this week, check out the Trapezium [*see #2*].) The doors of the school are always open to anyone who just wants to come and watch the fun. Arena seating makes it easy to stay a while. You don't need reservations, but it's a good idea to arrive when the school is at its busiest, usually Friday night and Saturday. An excellent playground nearby has an intricate, 30-foot rope-climbing structure that will give your children a chance to work off the energy built up by watching other kids.

If you don't live in Montréal, you may want to think about this seriously before you visit—there are true stories of families who have been forced to move here due to pressure from smitten children.

EATS FOR KIDS
Crescendo (5150 blvd. LaSalle, 514/766–217), right next door, has a beautiful terrace overlooking the river. They offer a standard kid's menu of chicken fingers, spaghetti, and burgers; and they have a children's brunch with breakfasts based on Disney characters.

GETTING THERE The school is right on the Lachine Canal Bike Path (*see #38*), so consider making this part of a bike trip. Coming from downtown you'll come to a fork just before the St. Paul lock. Follow the signs directing you south to Parc des Rapids. When you reach boulevard Champlain you'll meet another east/west bike path. Head east for a bit (DON'T head west along the boulevard Champlain aqueduct!), then head south on avenue Dupuis. Keep following the path until you reach the east/west waterfront trail. Head west. You can't miss the colourful arena. After your visit, keep biking west to see the rapids.

ÉCOMUSÉE DU FIER MONDE

In a 1920s art deco public bathhouse, you'll find this creative, elegant museum devoted to the history of Montréal's working-class neighbourhoods. It's a little off the beaten path, but well worth a visit. The photographs in the permanent exhibit are a stark contrast to the beautiful building. Life-size blowups of tenement children pushing their younger siblings in rusty strollers will no doubt make an impression, but overall this colourful exhibit will leave your children inspired.

The bathhouse was built to encourage hygiene in what was once one of the world's worst slums. Even Montrealers are shocked to learn about the Dickensian living conditions at the turn of the century. However, don't let this turn you off of bringing kids here. They'll walk through visuals from a century of dramatic social change, and sit down in a re-creation of a typical section of balconville, the word used to describe the architectural style that

EATS FOR KIDS Across the street is the Amherst market, a small farmer's market that has a health-food store with lots of brightly packaged organic treats. Or, you can find pizza, souvlaki, or a hamburger at the neighbourhood snack bar, **Deli-Kris** (2004 rue St-Hubert, 514/288-3589).

HEY, KIDS! Translated into English, *Fier Monde* means proud people. Montréal's working-class neighbourhoods have a lot to be proud of. In 1890 Montréal was the second-most-dangerous city in the world for children to live in, next to Calcutta. A child living here had only a three in four chance of making it to his or her fifth birthday. Now, not only is it one of the healthiest cities, Montréal students recently beat every country in the world, except Finland, on math tests.

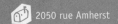 2050 rue Amherst

 $5 adults, $4 children 6–17

 W 11–8, Th–Su 10:30–5

514/528-8444,
www.fiermonde.cam.org

6 and up

encouraged families, stacked one on top of the other, to live on their outside stairwells. The fishnets of curiosities, mostly old and new toys hanging from the ceiling, show the care taken to make this exhibit kid-friendly. The temporary exhibit on the ground floor is usually angled for children as well. A typical example was Milk and the City, a history of milk promotion and production that included old cartons of Davy Crockett ice cream, a vintage milkman's uniform, and pictures of these mid-century heroes braving the fierce Montréal winters with icicles hanging from their crates of milk bottles.

After leaving, it's worth taking a stroll in the nearby blocks between rue Panet, rue de la Visitation, rue Ste-Catherine, and boulevard René-Lévesque. Most of the original triplexes remain and you can still see the *portes cochières,* the passageways through which residents drove their carriages into their tiny communal courtyards.

KEEP IN MIND This is one of the few Montréal museums that isn't bilingual. There is an English brochure available on request, but it doesn't give much detail. Fortunately, the visual appeal is such that children who don't speak French will still find it engaging. The temporary exhibits often include documentation, articles, and pamphlets written back when English was the official language. Judging from the many positive comments by Americans in the guest book, it's still quite accessible.

ECOMUSEUM

Wolves, black bears, caribou, falcons, otters, wild turkeys, ravens, and lynx are just some of the animals you'll find at this nonprofit wildlife preserve, less than 30 minutes from downtown. Most of the animals that live here have been orphaned or injured and can't return to the wild. Happily, the grassy, tranquil areas they live in are pretty close to their natural environment. If you have an aspiring vet in the family this is an ideal outing.

The first thing you'll see as you stroll along the pretty boardwalk flanked by green fields and ponds is Québec's official bird, the snowy owl. As you follow the path further you'll come to white-tailed deer, an arctic fox, a flying squirrel, and a couple of indignant wild turkeys. You should heed the signs that warn you to keep your distance from the turkeys: they've been known to bite. That doesn't mean you can't engage them in a bit of a debate, however. Shout "Hey, Turkeys!" and get ready for them to shout right back in unison, extending those red- and blue-veined gobblers to their fullest. Continue along the path

HEY, KIDS! Ravens are some of the smartest birds around. In Amerindian folklore they are often associated with mischief and take the form of the Trickster Spirit. Unlike some of the birds you'll meet at the Ecomuseum, ravens are not birds of prey; they're scavengers. Ravens never kill animals themselves. Instead, they eat meat killed by other animals. If there's no meat around they'll eat berries, bugs, or just about anything. Another interesting thing about ravens is that they usually choose one mate for life. They can't sing, but boy can they make noise!

21125 chemin Sainte-Marie;
take Exit 41 off Rte. 40

514/457-9449,
www.ecomuseum.ca

$7 adults, $4 children 4–14

Daily 9–5; no entrance after 4PM

2 and up

through a pretty waterfowl pond and on to some of the more majestic animals: the caribou, bears, wolves, and coyotes. Next up are the otters. If you have younger children be prepared to budget a good 15 minutes for these natural entertainers—they're worth it!

The next section houses turtles, porcupines, raccoons, and, if your kids have the nerves for it, a snake pit. The path may seem to end back at the main lodge; head off to the right of the lodge, however, and you'll find the Birds of Prey exhibit, a must-see. The horned owl, red-tailed hawk, golden eagle, and screech owl are all here. They're properly manacled, but you should still remind your kids to keep their cool around these birds. They aren't crazy about loud noises, and don't respond as well to teasing as the turkeys.

EATS FOR KIDS
In nearby Île Perrot is **Smoked Meat Pete** (99 blvd. Grand, 514/425–6068). The smoked meat at this friendly restaurant is almost as legendary as **Schwartz's Deli** (*see* Plateau Mont-Royal), and they have arguably the best fries in Montréal. There's also plenty of picnic space at the museum.

KEEP IN MIND Consider letting your kids adopt an animal. Don't worry, this doesn't mean you have to bring it home. It only means that you make a fixed donation toward its upkeep. This entitles your child to a special after-hours tour during the summer, where she'll get a chance to talk to that animal's caretaker, and in some cases even pet the animal. Prices range from $15 for a raven or a blue-spotted salamander to $200 for a black bear or caribou. You'll receive a certificate of adoption and your child's name will be displayed on the Parent Board.

EXPORAIL

All Aboard! Exporail houses one of North America's most significant train collections and actually lives up to that overused phrase "fun for the entire family." If there are grandparents available for this outing make sure to bring them. They'll be as thrilled as any five year old, and a valuable source of anecdotal history.

Kids can peer at, and in many cases climb into, some of the oldest and most impressive trains ever built in Canada. There's Montréal's first streetcar, The Rocket; Canada's oldest passenger car; and Canada's oldest surviving steam locomotive. There's a luxury passenger train with red-velvet seats and curtains, and gilded sleeping cars; and a private car belonging to Sir William Van Horne, the original manager of the Canadian Pacific Railway. A mail-sorting car harks back to the days when mail was sorted en route; and there's even a travelling school-house train, complete with school room and teacher's quarters. This

EATS FOR KIDS The best place to picnic is the Circus Train, which has tables and chairs and a fun poster exhibit. For a full meal try **Jennina Pizzeria** (108 rue St-Pierre, 514/632–0150), or **Château Grec** (97 rue St-Pierre, 514/638–1782), which are both near the entrance to the museum.

GETTING THERE St-Constant is about a 40-minute drive from Montréal. Cross the Mercier Bridge and take Route 132 South and then Route 209 West. Of course there is a more fun way to get there—by train! The museum is next to the St-Constant station, so you can go any day, but on certain Sundays and Wednesdays there is a special Museum Express reserved just for families going to Exporail. The train switches rails to ride directly into the museum. You get plenty of warning before the train returns to Montréal about four hours later.

 110 rue St-Pierre, St-Constant

 450/632-2410, www.exporail.org

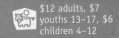 $12 adults, $7 youths 13–17, $6 children 4–12

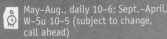 May–Aug., daily 10–6; Sept.–April, W–Su 10–5 (subject to change, call ahead)

 4 and up

train was built back when Ontario rural communities were so small and far apart, a teacher would arrive in a train that would stay for a week. There's also a now-extinct caboose with its office and observatory tower from the days when someone had to do the paperwork and surveillance that can now be done by computers.

Outside the main pavilion there are more trains and, of course, the all important train rides. You and your family can ride a 1920s streetcar, or ring the bell and sound the whistle in a 1960s passenger train. For kids from ages 4 to 94 there's the miniature railway—a small train with 6-foot-long cars—that takes a 10-minute ride around a figure-eight track with bridges and hills. Keep an eye out for days with special themes like railway ghosts or model-train enthusiasts. Expect to spend the whole day here as there's a lot of ground to cover. And don't forget your camera!

HEY, KIDS! In 1792 it took almost 17 days to get from Montréal to New York by horse-drawn carriage. The first train ride between the two cities took three days; now it takes about 10 hours. Bombardier, the same Montréal company that makes our quiet subways, is working on a high-speed train that would connect Montréal to Boston, Toronto, and New York. One day soon it may be possible to take a train to any of these cities in just a few hours. So maybe the era of train travel isn't quite over yet.

FIREFIGHTERS' MUSEUM

Judging from all the pictures you'll see here of firefighters dripping with icicles, Montréal may seem like one of the worst cities in the world for this job. Add to that the number of old buildings, and the statistically high number of smokers compared to other cities, and you can see that your average Montréal firefighter is usually a pretty experienced professional. Frosty the fireman is one of the many curiosities in this charming museum, but the thing kids seem to love most about this outing is the chance to question a firefighter tour guide about his job.

Housed in a beautiful old firehouse on the most elegant street in Montréal's Mile End district, this is an idyllic Sunday afternoon outing. A stroll along avenue Laurier is something a turn-of-the-century family might well have done back when this corner wasn't even in Montréal. It was part of the city of St. Louis until the early 20th century, and this

EATS FOR KIDS This is an excellent opportunity to visit the nearby **St-Viateur Bagel Factory** (see #9). Or, head east to **Chez Claudette** (351 av. Laurier Est, 514/279–5173), a friendly, funky, 24-hour diner that serves excellent *poutine*, Québec's official guilty-pleasure mixture of French fries, cheese, and gravy. This is a great place for young kids because they have crayons and colouring books. For something more elegant head to **Patisserie de Gascogne** (237 av. Laurier Ouest, 514/490–0235) for scrumptious sandwiches and mouth-watering pastries.

 5100 rue St-Laurent

 Free

 Su 1:30–4

 514/872–3757,
www.museedespompiers.com

 2 and up

was the St. Louis firehouse. It's easy to imagine the vintage 1890 horse-drawn steam engine reeling out of the coach house. What's harder to imagine is any fire actually being put out by the vintage fire equipment, like the hand pump and water barrel. It's no wonder so few of Montréal's original buildings remain.

Six other vintage fire vehicles, including a 1922 Seagrave Pumper and a 1952 Fargo Hosewagon, make this museum worth the trip. There's also an impressive collection of firefighting helmets from across North America and Europe. As an added bonus this museum shares the building with Fire Station 30, an actual working station. So if you're lucky—or someone else is unlucky—your kids may actually witness fire trucks leaving for a call.

KEEP IN MIND If your kids enjoy this outing, they might like a visit to the Police Cavalry Stables on Mont-Royal (see Beaver Lake). Neither of these outings take long, and Mont-Royal Park isn't far away, so you could do both on the same day. Just make sure you call the stables to reserve ahead.

HEY, KIDS! Those fireman dripping with icicles look pretty miserable, don't they? If you ask your guide if the cold is the worst thing about being a firefighter in Montréal you'll be surprised by the answer. Firemen actually love it when the weather is cold. The ice cools them down and keeps them insulated from the heat. So if you're visiting from out of town, and plan on being a fireman when you grow up, you might want to think about moving here!

FORT ANGRIGNON

ort Angrignon was once the winter home to animals from a zoo in Parc Lafontaine. The zoo no longer exists, but the cages at Fort Angrignon are still occupied; only now they're crawling with kids! All year round, you'll find teams of 8 to 12 kids and adults making their way through 15 Plexiglas rooms, each of which offers a different physical or intellectual challenge.

Wacky, energetic guides dressed up in leopard-print safari gear get your adrenaline pumped up for the two-and-a-half hour race ahead. One of the most difficult challenges is *La Turbine Chinoise* (The Chinese Harness). Kids have to place long rods into holders in a table without hitting the ceiling, and to make it extra tough, teams lose points for making noise. The most notorious challenge, however, is *Le Ventre de L'Araignée* (The Spider's Stomach). Participants must prove their courage by petting live tarantulas, scorpions, and lizards.

HEY, KIDS!
You'll have to pick a name for your team. You can pick something scary like the Spidermen, or the Scorpion Kings; think of something strong and smart like the Cougars; or, consider something that will get your team spirit going, like the Knights of (wherever you live).

KEEP IN MIND An excellent way to wind down from the inevitable pandemonium is a visit to the adjacent Angrignon Park. This is one of the largest wooded areas in the city. A great play area has a huge orange and purple spider web rope climbing gym. Head to the corner of boulevards des Trinitaires and de la Vérendrye and you'll find an interesting iron installation that frames the biggest lake like a landscape canvas. The nearby swampy areas are a good place to spot blue herons and red-winged blackbirds. In the summer, you'll find animals living nearby at the adjacent Little Farm at Angrignon Park (see #35).

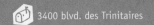 3400 blvd. des Trinitaires

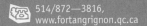 514/872—3816,
www.fortangrignon.qc.ca

 $13 adult, $10 youth
6–16, $6 child 4–6

 Sa–Su 10–5

 4 and up

The tarantulas aren't poisonous, and the scorpion has had his stinger removed. The lizards, however, are not all toilet trained, so there is a little risk involved.

Morning sessions at 10 AM are reserved for kids 4–5, accompanied by an adult. The race is an hour shorter, and the teams are smaller so if you're going with young kids you only need to put together a group of five or six. Prices for adults are reduced to $8 for these sessions. The standard challenge, offered for adults and older kids (6 and up), is available for two sessions, noon and 2:30. You have to put together your own team of 8 to 12 players. This is an extremely popular birthday party event, and reservations should be made at least a month in advance. The fact that this is run by a nonprofit group, which never advertises but is always booked, is pretty good testimony to how much fun it is.

EATS FOR KIDS There's a snack bar and indoor picnic tables at Fort Angrignon. You're welcome to bring your own food, or to order in. A popular place for take out is the nearby **Pizza Hut** (see Aquadôme). There are also outdoor picnic tables at the Little Farm, and Angrignon Park is a wonderful place for a picnic. If you're looking for a family restaurant, you'll find plenty to choose from along boulevard Newman, or you can try **Boccacino's** (see Little Farm at Angrignon Park).

THE FUR TRADE AT LACHINE NATIONAL HISTORIC SITE

At the end of the Lachine Canal bike path is a fun little museum devoted to *les voyageurs*, canoe couriers who took on the job of transporting fur pelts in Montréal's early years. These adventurous men are to Montréal what cowboys are to the Wild West. Their six-month trips west into the interior of Canada and then back to Montréal made the city the fur-trading capital of North America at a time when fur was a major and profitable export.

The museum is housed in a stone warehouse built in 1803. One of the main attractions for kids is the chance to stroke a number of luxurious wild-animal pelts. Deer, beaver, raccoon, mink, muskrat, otter, and fox don't tend to stay still for a petting zoo, so this is a rare chance to find out what they feel like. Kids will learn how important fur was to European fashions of the time, and how beaver pelts were made into top hats. They'll even get to check out how they look in these fashions. There are also displays about the

HEY, KIDS! You probably know the Mad Hatter from the story of *Alice in Wonderland*. You may even have heard the expression "mad as a hatter." In the 19th century, hatters used a dangerous chemical to make beaver fur more like felt. They ended up with symptoms like shaking hands and slurring words that made them seem a little crazy, hence the expression. Fortunately, that chemical isn't used any more. Most of the hats here are made of wool, but if you ask a guide you can see a real beaver top hat. It's worth about $400, so they keep it locked up.

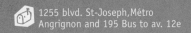

1255 blvd. St-Joseph, Métro
Angrignon and 195 Bus to av. 12e

514/637-7433,
www.parkscanada.gc.ca/fourrure

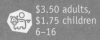
$3.50 adults,
$1.75 children
6–16

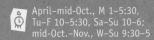
April–mid-Oct., M 1–5:30,
Tu–F 10–5:30, Sa–Su 10–6;
mid-Oct.–Nov., W–Su 9:30–5

7 and up

importance of Native Americans to the fur trade, and of course about the lives of
les voyageurs.

To be a good voyageur you had to be strong enough to haul two or three heavy
fur bales on a *portage*, which is when canoes had to be carried across land to
avoid rapids. You had to be savvy enough to negotiate with natives, crazy enough
to risk bad weather, and small enough to not take up too much room in the
canoe. Kids can step on a scale that will assure most of them that they are
under the 178 cm (5' 7") and 63 kg (140 lb) cut-off point. If you're at the
museum during one of the free tours, there's a good 20-minute documentary
that dramatizes this life.

EATS FOR KIDS
Café L'Ancrage (500 chemin
des Iroquois, 514/364–1290),
at the nearby Lachine Canal
National Historic Site, has
scrumptious sandwiches and a
great terrace overlooking the end
of the canal. **La Strada** (600 blvd.
St-Joseph, 514/637–3046) across
the street has good pastas and other
Italian specialties.

KEEP IN MIND Just east of the museum, the Lachine Canal Historic
Site has an interesting, free photographic exhibit about the history of the canal. West
of the museum, you can stroll along the original brick walls of the canal to Parc
René Lévesque. There's a magical sculpture garden here and a splendid view. Be
careful when crossing the bike path on foot. There are a number of curves and
blind spots on the path as it winds around the park.

GOLDEN SQUARE MILE

Are you having a hard time tearing a Lemony Snicket fan away from *A Series of Unfortunate Events*? Try offering a real-life adventure with a walk through the steep, lush, winding upper reaches of the Golden Square Mile. Some of the Gothic–Victorian mansions that overlook the city from the slope of Mont-Royal are now government embassies and pavilions in McGill's faculty of medicine. On weekends they stand vacant and mysterious, ready to ignite any child's imagination.

A walk up to the corner of rue Peel and avenue des Pins will leave most people out of breath, but the spectacular view of Montréal is worth it. Walk through the wrought-iron gateway at the northeast corner of rue Peel, up to the door of Ravenscrag. This sprawling mansion, named after a Scottish castle, was built in 1863 by Hugh Allan, a shipping magnate who used to keep an eye on his vessels from the watchtower. Remind your children that it was built before cars or electricity and watch their jaws drop. In 1943 it became the Allan Memorial Institute of Psychiatry.

GETTING THERE The least-steep route is to go up rue McTavish, then turn left on avenue des Pins. It's longer than walking up rue Peel, but easier for young children. You can also take the 144 Bus from Métro Sherbrooke to the corner of rue Peel and avenue des Pins.

HEY, KIDS! Avenue Docteur Penfield is named after Dr. Wilder Penfield. Before he died in 1976 he was once called "the greatest living Canadian." Actually, he was American, but he moved here early in his career to found the Montréal Neurological Institute at McGill University, and pursue his dream of building a team of brain surgeons who would revolutionize medicine. One of the really cool things he discovered was that if you stimulated a part of the brain over and over again, a person would experience the same memory. This discovery made it possible for him to create a map of the brain.

Walk west along avenue des Pins, past other towering, eclectic homes, and you'll come to Maison Cormier (#1418), the lovely art-deco mansion belonging to the Trudeau family. Across the street is the Cuban Consulate (#1415). Walk four houses back and descend the stairs leading down to the three intriguing mansions that make up the Russian Consulate on avenue du Musée.

From there you can backtrack, continue mansion hunting, or head up to Parc du Mont-Royal. Or, you can turn right on avenue Docteur Penfield and walk to a glamorous dog run on the corner of Redpath. Donated to the city by a wealthy dog lover, privileged dogs frolic happily up and down the steep, grassy inclines of Sir Walter Percy Park. The dog people here are usually friendly and happy to talk about their gorgeous pooches.

EATS FOR KIDS Walk through the parking lot behind the Allan Memorial and you'll find yourself in Jeanne Mance Park, a great place for a picnic. If your kids are in good shape, head to the Peel entrance of Parc du Mont-Royal, and then up the stairs that will bring you directly to the **Chalet** snack bar (see #66). Head down to rue Sherbrooke, and you can go for high tea at the **Ritz** (see #48), or grab a burger at the **Hard Rock Café** (1458 rue Crescent, 514/987–1420).

HIGH TEA IN THE RITZ GARDEN

Don't be put off by the lofty reputation of the Ritz-Carlton chain. The Montréal Ritz was the first one built in North America and was specifically designed for guests of the families living in the Golden Square Mile at the turn of the century. Kids are not only welcome for high tea, they have their own version. The Angel's Tea includes hot chocolate and their own selection of pastries. Of course kids love it. What is this ritual, but an adult version of milk and cookies?

Tea is served year-round, but the best place for kids is the Ritz Garden, open in the warmer months. Spend a little time exploring the lobby, especially if you're bringing a daughter. The Ritz first opened its doors for a New Year's Eve ball in 1912. The winding gold staircase was designed by Oscar Ritz to show off the gowns of female guests. Check out the Palm court, so named for the potted palms that add that British–Colonialist touch, and the gorgeous chandeliers in the ballroom.

HEY, KIDS! You'll want to use your best manners at the Ritz, but don't worry if you drop your spoon. Worse has happened. Elwood Bigelow Hosmer inherited a majority share of the Ritz from his father in 1927. When the Great Depression hit the hotel hard, Hosmer wasn't much help. Nicknamed "The Grey Ghost of the Ritz," he drank too much, insulted the guests, and once he even peed on one of the trees in the Palm Court! "Being president of the company didn't matter," a worker told the hotel's official biographer, "the moment Mr. Hosmer became a bloody nuisance, out the door he went!"

 1228 rue Sherbrooke Ouest

 $26 adult tea, $9.50 angel's tea

514/842-1212,
www.ritzcarlton.com

 Daily 3:30–5

 5–17

Adult tea service is appropriately swank, with scones and Devonshire cream, carefully crafted finger sandwiches, and pastries served on a tri-level silver tray. The great thing about this outing is that it acquaints children with the experience of formal dining without all the stress and boredom of waiting in between courses. If they get restless, there's the duck pond in the garden to explore, and of course there are always people to watch on this affluent-neighbourhood terrace: brides being photographed, couples in walking shorts dropping by after some afternoon shopping, and maybe even a celebrity. Though they're unlikely to see the Queen of England (who, when she's here, usually has her tea in the Royal Suite), older kids may be fans of recent guests, the Backstreet Boys.

EATS FOR KIDS
If all goes well, you might want to try a dinner in **Le Café de Paris.** The food is excellent, and the Ritz's children's menu includes a Pokémon hamburger, spaghetti, and a peanut-butter and jelly sandwich.

KEEP IN MIND If you really want to go for the royal treatment, you could book a room. Children under two are presented with Leland the Ritz Lion. Children 2-12 get Carlton, the Ritz beanie baby. They also get unlimited Nintendo and are served milk and cookies in their room every afternoon. If you want to go out, the hotel provides baby-sitting on request. If this isn't in your budget (high season packages start at $395 a night), you can purchase Leland or Carlton in the gift shop.

HORIZON ROC

Now that there seems to be a rock-climbing wall in just about every shopping centre, you may wonder why you should trek out to the east end of the city, past the Olympic Stadium, for this popular sport. When you arrive you'll understand—this is no ordinary rock-climbing wall; this may be the biggest indoor rock-climbing centre in the world. In addition to the 25,000 square feet of climbing space, there's a specially designed children's section to accommodate kids as young as three, a competition-size artificial boulder, and a children's play area inside the boulder.

If there's a rock-climbing centre that can boast more climbing space than this one the enthusiastic staff at Horizon Roc doesn't know about it yet. Open since 1994, major renovations in 2003 have almost doubled its size from the original 15,000 square feet. Just sitting around in the mezzanine lounge, watching the walls covered with crawling humans, is worth the trip.

KEEP IN MIND Trial sessions have to be reserved in advance. The centre will provide supervisors for children 5 and older. If you have children who are 3 or 4, they can only climb if you supervise them yourself, and you have to be a certified climber to do this.

EATS FOR KIDS Head up to rue Sherbrooke and you'll find masses of well-known family-style restaurants. At **Nickels** (5460 rue Sherbrooke Est, 514/259–6937) you'll notice a big sign that says KIDS EAT FOR FREE! This is great for kids, but it means you have to eat the adult food, which is average at best. Adventurous families might like to try **Jardin Tiki** (5300 rue Sherbrooke Est, 514/254–4173), a fabulously kitschy Polynesian-style restaurant with a massive all-you-can-eat buffet. You have to cross a bridge over live turtles to get to your table, and there's a self-serve soft-ice-cream machine!

2350 rue Dickson,
near Métro L'Assomption

Trial session $12 per
person; $9 per person for
groups of 3 or more

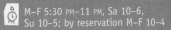
M–F 5:30 PM–11 PM, Sa 10–6,
Su 10–5; by reservation M–F 10–4

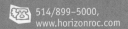
514/899–5000,
www.horizonroc.com

3 and up

If you've never done this before, your family can do a 90-minute trial session. If you decide to make this a regular outing adults can take a three-hour course to be certified. Older kids, ages 10–13, have several courses specially designed for them. Younger kids, ages 5–9, don't have courses, but they can join a supervised club *Les Petits Lézards (The Little Lizards)* that meets for 90 minutes each week. Kids can climb in the supervised kids' area any time during opening hours. Cute animals, caves, slides, and slanted walls make it more kid-friendly than the adult section.

If you and your kids are climbing together, be sure to leave any alpha-parent attitude at home. Kids tend to be light, flexible, and full of energy, all of which means climbing is easier for them. You may be eating your kids dust—or chalk—before you know it.

HEY, KIDS! The first thing you'll probably notice when you walk into Horizon Roc is all the pretty colours. It sure looks groovy, but this isn't someone's great decorating idea. Those colours map out different routes climbers have to complete. Different colours mean different degrees of difficulty. There are over 200 routes mapped out here, and they change them all the time. So even if you're a natural climber, you don't ever have to worry about getting bored.

ÎLE-DE-LA-VISITATION NATURE PARK

46

When the earliest French settlers decided enough lives had been lost to the Iroquois, they briefly relocated their military fort to Montréal's north shore, at what is now Île-de-la-Visitation Nature Park (which, despite its name, is not actually an island). After finding themselves just as vulnerable, however, the majority of settlers returned south. Four hundred years later, it's Montréal's summer crowds you may want to flee.

Those few settlers who remained on the north shore took advantage of the rapids to power a mill. The foundation of this mill, Maison du Meunier, is at the west entrance of the park. Not far from the mill, children can visit Maison du Pressoir, a reconstructed 18th-century-cider brewery. On summer weekends, tour guides wander around in period costume. Keep in mind, however, in this neck of the woods few are fluent in English.

Along the forested shoreline, kids can walk down to watch amateur fishermen casting their bait into the largest spawning ground in Southern Québec. Remember to be vigilant here

GETTING THERE The park is a 15-minute walk east along boulevard Gouin from Métro Henri-Bourrasa, making the Métro the easiest way to get here. Another option is the Christophe Colombe bike path that runs from the south shore to the north. If you rent bikes in the Old Port (see #21) this will take a good hour, which may be too long for little legs. It's better to rent your bikes at Maison des Cyclists (see #34) which will cut the trip in half; or bring your bikes on the Métro. There is a 2.5-km (1.5-mi) bike path in the park, making this a great alternative to the often overcrowded Lachine Canal Bike Path.

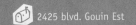
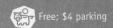

as the rapids can be dangerous. Eventually you'll reach a bridge which leads to a wooden gazebo that overlooks the area where the river roars into a reservoir that powers an impressive hydroelectric dam. Walk (or if it's winter, cross-country ski) back across the bridge and continue along the shore to the other side of the dam where you'll discover more rapids, beaches, another arresting view from another gazebo, and a nice little toddler playground. Keep an eye out for a graceful community of herons.

Leave some time to visit the nearby Église de la Visitation, the oldest church in Montréal. And don't forget to stop by the graveyard on the corner of boulevard Henri-Bourassa and avenue Papineau; here you'll see some of the trails the Iroquois used for their nighttime attacks.

EATS FOR KIDS
There are many spots to picnic, or you can grab something at the snack bar in the main chalet. It may be hard, however, to resist sandwiches at the **Bistro-Terrasse des Moulins** (514/280-6709), in La Maison du Meunier interpretation centre. It overlooks a pretty stretch of rapids.

HEY, KIDS! When you're walking along the forested area of the shore you'll notice chicken wire wrapped around the base of the tall trees. What do you think they're being protected from? Curious dogs? Nope. Rogue beavers have been known to gnaw down these trees to build dams. You may even see one! Since the hydro station can occasionally open its gates and flood the area in under a minute, the chicken wire not only protects the trees, it keeps the beavers from building dams where they might end up drowning.

IMAX AT THE OLD PORT

I f your thrill-seeking child has dragged you to one preposterous action film too many, the IMAX theatre at the Old Port is the perfect compromise for your next movie outing. This theatre shows 45-minute films on a seven-story screen, amplified with 15,000 watts of sound. You're guaranteed a hair-raising action documentary free of silly plots, inane acting, and wooden dialogue.

A typical example is *Top Speed*, narrated by Tim Allen, which focuses on the human pursuit of extreme acceleration. Follow the first major race of a young race-car driver who's been speeding since he was old enough to drive a go-cart. Ride on the handlebars of a 37-year-old female mountain-bike racer as she bikes down the icy Olympic bobsled track in Salt Lake City; then get a bird's-eye view from inside the world's fastest off-road vehicle as it speeds toward a cliff in Colorado. No doubt you and your kids will be gripping the comfy padded armrest in the steep stadium seats.

EATS FOR KIDS Zoomatic, in the lobby of the IMAX theatre, is part gift shop and part cafeteria-style restaurant with a good selection of sandwiches, soups, and salads. There's also an overwhelming number of plush animal toys and a terrace that overlooks the waterfront.

HEY, KIDS! Did you know that IMAX was invented in Canada? It was created to film Canadian geography, since ordinary film technology couldn't quite capture the awesome northern landscape. The first permanent IMAX theatre was in Ontario Place in Toronto, and the first IMAX feature was *North of Superior*, produced in 1971. This 18-minute tribute to the beautiful Canadian North was filmed on rafts in white-water rapids and from planes travelling across cliffs and lakes. It climaxed with shots of a raging forest fire that seemed to engulf the audience.

 King Edward Pier

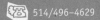 514/496-4629

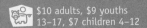 $10 adults, $9 youths
13–17, $7 children 4–12

 Daily 10 AM–8:30 PM

7 and up

Fortunately, breathers between action sequences come in the form of some interesting educational facts and human-interest stories. For instance, *Top Speed* also follows the career of Marion Jones, the Olympic Gold Medal sprinter, and her intense training that involves a surprising amount of very slow yoga and meditation. If you're looking for something more appropriate for younger children, or children who have a lower thrill threshold, there's usually a second movie with more of an educational, or exploration theme. Children under the age of three, however, must sit on your lap for the entire film to literally keep them from jumping out of their seats. Don't think you can bypass this rule by buying them their own seat. Breaking this rule can get you kicked out, so unless it's your toddler's nap time, you might not want to risk this.

KEEP IN MIND After watching all this action, your kids may be ready for some adventures of their own. There are plenty of thrills down at the Old Port (*see #21*). Head over to the Clock Tower Pier and watch the speed boat rides, for instance. Ask what's happening at the information booth. Every summer new activities—from rock climbing to trapeze trials—are featured on the roster. If you're looking for a more educational outing, the IMAX offers a package deal that includes a visit to the Montréal Science Centre (*see #27*).

INSECTARIUM

44

Built to resemble a giant fly, this is the largest insect museum in North America. On first sight, even kids who aren't obsessed with Spiderman will be buzzing with curiosity. Take your time browsing the interactive exhibit in the lobby. Here you and your kids will get some fun scientific background: look at the world through an insect's eyes, broken up into dozens of fragments so that movement is easier to detect; or compare your strength with the relative strength of a bug—even the most jaded 10-year-old will be impressed.

The main exhibit downstairs is divided into six zones. You don't want to bore kids with the bugs they know best, so start with the Neotropical zone where they'll see beetles as large as hamsters and exquisite green and gold beetles used for jewelry. Next over is the Oriental zone where they'll learn how insects are used for clothes and entertainment. The Rhinoceros beetles, for example, are the stars of public combats and are sold on the street for the price of a coke. The Australian zone has the most beautiful butterflies. In the Ethiopian

KEEP IN MIND If you're here in early winter don't miss the insect tastings where highly trained chefs prepare unique treats from around the world: chocolate-covered grasshoppers, ant cakes, Tunisian meal worms, and spicy scorpions. The weekend is more for family tastings, whereas weeknights cater to the happy-hour crowd. Between February and May, there's Butterflies Go Free, a magical event, especially for young children. Hundreds of tropical butterflies are cultivated and allowed to roam freely in a room at the nearby Botanical Garden (see #29). Bring a camera. You don't want to miss your child's face when an electric blue Morpho Peleides lands on her shoulder.

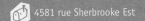 4581 rue Sherbrooke Est

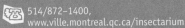 514/872-1400,
www.ville.montreal.qc.ca/insectarium

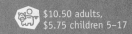 $10.50 adults,
$5.75 children 5–17

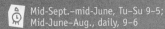 Mid-Sept.–mid-June, Tu–Su 9–5;
Mid-June–Aug., daily, 9–6

 4 and up

zone there's the giraffe weevil, so called for its long neck, and the Madagascar cockroach, which hisses like a snake to scare off predators. Obviously, the Palearctic zone is the smallest. By the time you get to our zone, the Neararctic, some children may be feeling their lives are relatively bug impoverished.

Don't worry too much about budgeting time; even the biggest bug collection doesn't take up much space. Leave yourself at least 10 minutes to check out the short documentary by George Brossard, who collected most of these specimens. An eccentric Montréal adventurer who's a little like the Crocodile Hunter of the insect planet, Brossard explains the role of insects in South American creation myths, picks up killer ants with tweezers and scorpions with his fingers, and is led blind by an Indian tribe through the stinging-ant initiation ritual.

EATS FOR KIDS

The Insectarium is part of the Botanical Garden (*see #29*) complex. It's forbidden to picnic on the grounds here, but there are picnic tables just outside the rue Viau entrance. In the summer **Le Pavillon Fuji** is a pretty outdoor snack bar; in the colder months the **Garden Snack Bar** has a good selection of food.

HEY, KIDS! Did you know that bugs are nutritious? They're a great source of lipids, vitamins, and minerals, and have tons of protein. This makes sense when you think about it. Bugs are one of the most important food sources for animals. Cooked properly, many people from other continents consider them a treat. But don't eat them unless they've been cleaned and prepared by a qualified bug chef!

JARRY PARK

43

Ask most Montrealers to recommend a park and it's unlikely you'll hear Jarry Park mentioned very often. Unfairly perceived as being a little *too* off the beaten track, Jarry Park is surprisingly accessible by two Métro lines. Though much smaller than megaparks like Mont-Royal and Jean-Drapeau, it offers a remarkable variety of activities, and boasts a man-made lake far prettier than the much more popular Beaver Lake. If that weren't enough, the park is only a 10-minute walk from Jean Talon Market (*see #42*), which means you can plan an exceptional family picnic without having to prepare any food.

Head to the northeast corner of the park to visit the mammoth-sized toddler wading pool. Three great fountains, the largest resembling a gigantic, red, sea snake, spray kids with water—keeping them entertained and the pool super clean. Next to the pool are two well-equipped playgrounds. Almost everything in the preschool playground faces the morning sun, so bring shades and hats.

KEEP IN MIND One of the best times to visit is the first weekend of June for the Tour de l'Île des Enfants, Montréal's bike race for kids (*see Maison des Cyclists*). Jarry Park is the finish line, so even if your kids aren't in the race, they can cheer the participants as they arrive.

EATS FOR KIDS If you're interested in a culinary adventure, consider breakfast at **Melchorita** (7901 rue St-Dominique, 514/382–2129). This very authentic Peruvian restaurant serves up a unique family-style breakfast. One order serves four and comes with delicious chunks of pork, sausage, perfect egg-stuffed tamales, and sweet-potato chips that are usually a hit with kids. In the afternoon there's roasted chicken and empañadas. If you're really adventurous try the purple *chincha morada*, a corn drink invented by the Incas. For more traditional American food, there's always nearby **McDonald's** (7275 blvd. St-Laurent, 514/276–6878).

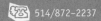 Off blvd. St-Laurent at rue Jarry, Métros Jarry and De Castelneau

 Free

 Daily 6 AM–12 AM

514/872-2237

 All ages

Older kids will find more of interest in the northwest corner of the park, including volleyball nets, a skateboarding half pipe, a roller-hockey rink, three baseball diamonds, three soccer fields, and even a cricket field. In the southeast corner there's a public pool, but most impressive is the lake. Landscaped with bulrushes, weeping willows, and poplars, rogue herons fly into the city on quiet mornings just to hang out here. In the winter it freezes over for skating.

If you're a tennis family, consider booking a court at the nearby Du Maurier Stadium, which has the least-expensive outdoor ($10/hr) and indoor ($15) courts in the city (reservations 514/273-1234). Or book some seats for the Tennis Masters Canada tournament, which is attended by many of the world's top-seeded players, and is usually held in mid-August. Just don't expect to play tennis while the tournament is on.

HEY, KIDS! Next to the wading pool is the Pavilion John Paul II. This was named for the Pope who gave a huge Catholic mass in the park in 1986. Next to the pavilion you'll see a big sculpture that looks like a pair of wings. This was built in 1991. Kids in Montréal were asked to donate all their war toys as a way of praying for world peace. These toys were buried under the sculpture, and some of them were bronzed and built into the sculpture. Only two remain, a tank and a pistol. Can you spot them?

JEAN TALON MARKET

42

Montréal has several excellent farmers' markets, but Jean Talon is its biggest and best. A kaleidoscope of brightly coloured vegetables might be a certain kid's nightmare, but there are lots of treats here to keep children curious—maple syrup, cranberry candy, mouthwatering bakeries, and pastry and cheese shops that may convert even the most stubborn child into a potential foodie.

Consider stopping first at **Première Moisson** bakery on the rue Casgrain side of the market. You might be surprised how a toddler who normally refuses crusts will be delighted by the texture of a perfectly baked, endlessly chewy baguette. Pick up some fresh curd cheese, or a chunk of St-Guillaume from **Fromagerie Hamel** on the boulevard Jean-Talon side. These have a mild taste, and squeaky texture that most kids adore. Avoid the line by grabbing them prepackaged next to the gigantic cheese wheels on the front counter.

HEY, KIDS! At **Marché des Saveurs** on the rue Mozart side of the market, you'll find all kinds of unusual food made in Québec. Check out the caribou pâté which is made in Nunavik, Québec's arctic region. This is a vast, beautiful territory—about 300,000 square miles, which is really big! There are so many lakes in Nunavik you can't even count them. There are also close to a million caribou, and as you can see, those containers are pretty small. So if you taste some you're not endangering the herd, you're helping the Inuit, Naskapi, and Cree people who live up there.

 7075 rue Casgrain, at blvd. Jean-Talon

 Free

 Daily 8–6

 514/277-1379, www.marchespublics-mtl.com

All ages

One of the most linguistically diverse spots in the city, the market is a feast for the ears as well as the eyes. Walk into **Poissonerie Shamrock,** a popular fish market (corner of rue Casgrain and rue Mozart), and you'll be greeted in Spanish. Next door at **Capitol** and **Chez Nino** you'll find the Italian community debating the best balsamic vinegar. A few doors down, European butchers compete with Arab butchers, both grilling meat outside their shops. Walk into **Sami Fruits**, on the boulevard Jean-Talon side of the market, and you'll get a great sense of what it must be like on market day in the Middle East. Look closely before you buy, however—what Sami offers in sheer bulk isn't always matched by quality. Consider buying from the more expensive fruit and vegetable shops like **Chez Nino** or **Chez Louis** (next to Nino), which supply Montréal's top restaurants. Your child may find himself biting into the most delicious grape, apple, peach, or even broccoli, he's ever tasted.

EATS FOR KIDS
If the weather turns bad, head to **Motta** (303 rue Mozart Est, 514/270–5952), an Italian bakery and restaurant which has a covered terrace. For something different, try **La Caretta** (350 rue St-Zotique Est, 514/278–5779) one block south. Kids love the soft tortilla *Pupusas* here.

GETTING THERE Weekend parking here is a nightmare. Fortunately, the market is two blocks from Métro Jean-Talon. Unfortunately, finding the right Métro exit can be confusing. Here's a tip: If you're coming from downtown on the orange line (direction Henri-Bourassa), turn right when you step off the Métro. When you go through the turnstiles you'll see a sign for Marché Jean-Talon, which will take you to boulevard Jean-Talon. Cross rue St-Denis, and walk two more blocks to the market. If you're coming by the blue line, head to the Henri-Bourassa platform and follow the above directions.

JET BOATING ON THE LACHINE RAPIDS

41

Visit a few Montréal museums and you'll hear all about the Lachine Rapids and how impossible they were for pioneers to navigate. Many kids will not be significantly impressed with this fact, but get them out there on those rapids and they'll come away with a whole new respect for the early settlers—not to mention sopping wet, and thrilled to the core.

The idea of heading into 13-foot waves in a jet boat with your kids may make you a little nervous. If you're not sure about your family's thrill threshold you may want to think this out a bit. Though there are extremely experienced jet-boating companies that operate tours from the Old Port, the boats are big and the rapids themselves are a little far from the starting point. **Rafting Montréal** operates out of the west end neighbourhood of LaSalle, right next to the rapids. The boats are smaller, and the experienced, friendly guides tailor the speed to a comfort and safety level appropriate for your kids. If anyone gets nauseous

HEY, KIDS!
La Chine is the French name for China. The rapids were named this to make fun of an early explorer and land owner, Robert Cavalier de La Salle. He was so obsessed with finding a passageway to China that Montréal residents called his territory La Chine, and the name stuck.

EATS FOR KIDS If you're driving, you can head up to boulevard Newman where there are many well-known, family-style restaurants (see Aquadôme.) If you're biking or taking public transport, **LaSalle Drive-In** (8760 blvd. LaSalle, 514/365–6700) is a good greasy spoon with picnic benches that overlook the rapids. If you're going on the late-afternoon run, ask about the combined rafting and dinner special which the company offers in conjunction with the nearby **Brasserie Des Rapides** (7852 blvd. Champlain, 514/595–3197).

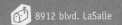 8912 blvd. LaSalle

 514/767-2230,
www.raftingmontreal.com

 $45 adults, $35 youths 13–18,
$25 children 8–12

 May–Sept., daily 9–6,
reservations essential

 8 and up

or scared, you're never more than a few minutes away from shore. Also you have the option of rafting, which is a less risky and more physically active choice (jet-boat trips will take kids as young as 8, and rafts will take kids as young as 6).

The jet-boat excursion starts with your family being zipped up into lightweight full-body windbreakers. Don't imagine for a second these will keep you dry. A full change of clothes, underwear, and shoes is an absolute must. Your captain and guide will start you out with a few sharp turns just to check everyone's comfort level, then you'll tackle increasingly bigger waves. The first time you get thoroughly drenched by a wave it's a total shock. The last time you get drenched by a wave, appropriately nicknamed the "nose washer," it's still a total shock. The shock wears off, but this is a trip you want to do in really warm-weather months, no matter what they tell you about being open from May to September.

GETTING THERE Driving from downtown (a 15-minute drive), take Highway 20, Exit 63 and then Exit 2, and follow the sign RAFTING SUR LE ST-LAURENT. By public transport take the 110 Bus from Métro Angrignon. Biking from the Old Port will take you a good hour. To cut the distance, take your bikes on the Métro, and then bike from Métro Angrignon, through Angrignon Park, along the aqueduct, to the waterfront trail. Bring a map, so you don't get lost and miss your reservation. **Rafting Montréal** has a shuttle that leaves the downtown Info-Touriste Centre in the afternoon. Phone for information.

JUST FOR LAUGHS MUSEUM

40

A comedy museum? A lot of laughter greeted this contradiction in terms when it was first built. Though it continues to get mixed reviews from adults, kids don't care about the clash between high and low culture. They just want to laugh, and there's a lot of that here—maybe too much.

On the top floor, the Abracadabra exhibit is specifically designed for kids ages 4 to 12. Toddlers may not understand what's going on, but they're welcome to tag along. Just keep a firm grip on them in the entrance hall of mirrors. Charming tour guides dressed up as magicians take you and your family through five different rooms devoted to the history and secrets of magic. In a brief History of Magic, kids will learn about the earliest evidence of the art in ancient Egypt, and about the magicians who were imprisoned as sorcerers. In The Gallery of the Impossible, they'll be turned into ghosts and mystified by a telescope that can see through solid objects. In the Gallery of Optical Illusions they'll

HEY, KIDS! At the Abracadabra exhibit you'll see a film clip of the famous Harry Houdini escaping from a metal box in Montréal's St. Lawrence River. Houdini is considered the father of modern-day magic. In the early 1900's he worked on Vaudeville with a family called the Keatons. Young Joseph Keaton was so fascinated with Houdini's magic that Houdini nicknamed him Buster. And so it is that one of film's most famous comedians got his name from one of magic's most-famous magicians.

2111 blvd. St-Laurent

514/845–4000,
www.hahaha.com

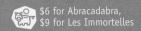$6 for Abracadabra,
$9 for Les Immortelles

Tu–F 9–5, Sa–Su 10–5

4–12 for Abracadabra; 10
and up for Les Immortelles

see more than two dozen different ways their own eyes can play tricks on them.
They'll be shown rope tricks, card tricks, and will even get to make their own flying
box in the Magician's Workshop. Elements of all these rooms are brought together
in a final magic show.

The downstairs exhibit, Les Immortelles, is more appropriate for older kids. This
is a bona fide comedian's hall of fame. In a huge neon-lit room filled with a
series of small theatres, comedy buffs can walk in and out of various 20-minute
films from different eras ranging from Buster Keaton to Jim Carrey. In total
there's about three hours of comedy sketches. If your children are really
obsessed, they can follow this up with a 2½-hour film of 100 classic sketches.
If they're still laughing, accept that you may be the parent of a budding
stand-up comedian.

EATS FOR KIDS
This is a great opportunity to
head above rue Sherbrooke to
discover Montréal's famous delis
(see Plateau Mont-Royal). Don't
head south or you'll soon end up
in the seediest and least kid-friendly
district of the city. There's also a
snack bar in the museum.

KEEP IN MIND The Just for Laughs Festival, which takes place every
year in mid-July, is widely considered the most important showcase for stand-up
comedy in the industry. It's also a great festival for kids. Clowns, acrobats, street
magicians, and people in just plain silly costumes wander daily throughout the festival area. The most popular event is the twin parade. Every year twins from all
over the world arrive to march in it. If you have twins you can find out about
joining at www.hahaha.com.

LABYRINTHE DU HANGAR

39

Here's a fun outing for a rainy, or potentially rainy, day. If plans to visit the Old Port or bike the Lachine Canal suddenly fall through, you can salvage the day by popping into this indoor maze built inside a 27,000-square-foot hangar. Just make sure everyone is well fed, well rested, and has had a recent trip to the bathroom. You don't want to be heading into this venture unprepared.

Each year the maze is redesigned and constructed around a story that usually has some kind of mysterious storage theme. One recent scenario starts with your family sitting down to watch a short video about Al Capone's regular visits to Montréal during prohibition. A fictional character named Omer has seen Capone hanging around the warehouse. Overly curious, Omer is now trapped inside the hangar and your job is to find and free him. To do

KEEP IN MIND This is the most physical indoor activity at the Old Port. If you're looking for something less stressful, there's the IMAX show (see #45), or try one of the kid-friendly museums like Point-à-Callière (see #12), Centre d'Histoire (see #60), Château Ramezay (see #58), or the Marguerite Bourgeoys Museum (see #32).

HEY, KIDS! Montréal has a history of shady warehouses. During prohibition in the 1920s, alcohol was illegal all over North America except here. Montréal was considered Canada's "sin city." Gangsters, however, weren't the only ones profiting. Outside the hangar you can see the clock built by the Molson family. They and the Bronfmans, who built important landmarks like the Canadian Centre of Architecture (see #63), both made their fortune from bootlegging. Today, Montréal has one of the lowest crime rates on the continent, and if you look around the Old Port you can see those shady-warehouse days are long gone.

 Old Port, Hangar 16

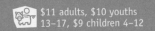 $11 adults, $10 youths 13–17, $9 children 4–12

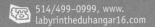 514/499–0999, www. labyrintheduhangar16.com

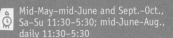 Mid-May–mid-June and Sept.–Oct., Sa–Su 11:30–5:30; mid-June–Aug., daily 11:30–5:30

 4 and up

this you must find other characters within the maze who will send you on scavenger hunts to earn passwords to yet other sections of the maze. Forests of elastic cords, storage drums that must be crawled under, and tunnel slides add an extra physical challenge.

The entire game should take you an hour to 90 minutes, depending on luck, sense of direction, and honesty. Technically you're supposed to be expelled for cheating by crawling under the vinyl flaps that act as walls, but the friendly staff is easily charmed into giving shortcuts and hints. There's also a break area in between two sections of the maze where you can take a breather. Just be warned: for mysterious reasons children are much, much better at this than adults, so don't feel like you have to take the lead in getting your kids through this. Concentrate instead on keeping up with them.

EATS FOR KIDS When it rains many of the stalls along rue de la Commune shut down. You can still get a good meal at the restaurant in the Jacques Cartier Pavilion (see Old Port of Montréal), or head up to Place Jacques Cartier to **Jardin Nelson** (see Château Ramezay). **Harvey's** (452 Pl. Jacques Cartier, 514/875–6379) has better than average fast food if you're looking for a quick, cheap bite. If the weather clears up they have a surprisingly excellent terrace.

LACHINE CANAL BIKE PATH

Of the roughly 350 km (217 mi) of bike trails on the island of Montréal, this trail is by far the most popular. The flat paved 11-km (7-mi) waterfront path has one long beautiful view of the city skyline. It's bordered by parkland where you can picnic or take a break, and it's accessible from a number of neighbourhoods and Métro stops. Several scenic and fun detours add another 30 km (19 mi) of paths, and since 2002 bikers can also include boating on their adventure (see #37).

The Old Port is the best place to rent bikes (see #21) and it should take your family about two hours to bike from here to the other end of the trail. The first section, which runs between the Old Port and the Peel Basin, is the busiest, especially on sunny summer weekends. If your children aren't too young or skittish, keep heading west and the crowd will thin

KEEP IN MIND Bikes are allowed on the Métro all weekend, all day on holidays, and from 10 AM to 3 PM and 7 PM to 12 AM on weekdays. You must use the first car, and only four bikes are allowed in this car at one time. Bikes are not allowed on evenings when there are fireworks, or on Grand Prix weekends, when the Métro is unusually crowded. If you're driving there are several parking lots along the way. Call or pick up a map at Centre Info-Touriste at Dorchester Square (514/873-2015, bordered by rue Peel and blvd. René-Lévesque).

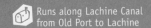 Runs along Lachine Canal from Old Port to Lachine

 Free

 514/283-6054, www.parcscanada.gc.ca/canallachine

 Daily 24 hrs

 All ages

out some. As you approach the Saint-Gabriel lock you may see guides dressed up as *les Filles du Roi* (the King's Wards), hoping to lure you to visit Maison Saint-Gabriel (*see #33*). By all means heed their siren call, especially if it's Sunday.

If you prefer to avoid the crowd, you can hop the Métro to the Lionel Groulx station. From there bike a few minutes down rue Atwater passed the Atwater Market to the canal. This is the place to look into renting boats (*see #37*). From here you can take a detour to École de Cirque de Verdun (*see #56*) and on to the spectacular Lachine Rapids. Or, you can continue along the canal path until you reach beautiful René Lévesque Park, where you can visit the Fur Trade at Lachine National Historic Site (*see #50*).

EATS FOR KIDS

Café America (20 rue des Seigneurs, 514/937–9983), right on the trail near the St-Gabriel Lock, is a high-quality cafeteria-style restaurant with everything from sandwiches to four-course specials. For a true food adventure, the **Atwater Market** is the second-largest farmer's market in the city (*see Lachine Canal Boat Tours*).

HEY, KIDS! Accidents definitely happen on this bike trail, so here are some safety guidelines you should keep in mind: Make sure your helmet is level on your head; if you look up you should be able to see the front edge. It's also a good idea to have a bell on your bike and to ring it when you're going through the little tunnels on the path. Don't speed through these tunnels—you never know when someone might be coming through from the other side.

LACHINE CANAL BOAT TOURS

Boating along the Lachine Canal is a serene and unique, unhurried way to take in the city. When it opened in 1825, the canal was used to bypass the treacherous Lachine Rapids, making the industrialization of Montréal possible. Now the area is a scenic waterfront park, extremely popular for cycling (*see #38*). It's only recently, since 2002, that leisure boating has been allowed, turning this 11-km (7-mi) ribbon of water into one of Montréal's major highlights.

Very low speed limits, 10 kph (6 mph) on private boats, make it safe to take children of all ages onto the water in anything from a pedal boat to a kayak. If your family is athletic you can turn a bike trip into an instant biathlon. **Ca Roule** (*see #21*) offers bike and boat-rental packages.

EATS FOR KIDS A snack bar serves ice cream and sandwiches at the Atwater dock. For picnic food head to the nearby **Atwater Market** (140 rue Atwater). **William J Walter** (south end, indoor, 514/933–4070) makes great low-fat-sausage sandwiches. If you want to sit down, nearby **Pizzancora** (514/935–0333) makes excellent pizza.

KEEP IN MIND Your kids will no doubt notice *L'Eclusier*, a glass-ceilinged, Parisian-style bateau-mouche at the Atwater dock. This hour-long cruise run by Parks Canada and narrated by one of their rangers is an interesting history lesson for adults, but after 20 minutes most kids will be clawing to get out. The cruise is excruciatingly slow and about the only thing of interest to kids is the novelty of going through the locks. *L'Eclusier* must wait until all other boats are out of the lock before leaving, which makes this just a little bit more fun than waiting in line at customs.

 South of Atwater Market

 $6–$43 per hr

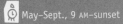 May–Sept., 9 AM–sunset

 514/938–4448 for Rubanbleu, www.rubanbleu.ca

 All ages

For a pleasant, undemanding, self-guided cruise, head just south of the Atwater Market to the blue and white fleet of boats rented out by **Ruban Bleu**. Here you can rent two- to four-seat pedal boats or single or double kayaks. Or you can rent one of their ingenious motor boats: These fiberglass electric boats with submerged motors make no noise or wake and will accommodate a group of five or seven. The largest has a picnic table.

For something more physically challenging, head further west to the dock at rue Monk and rue St-Patrick. **H2O Adventures** has a fleet of 15 sleek performance kayaks ($15/hr, $10/ additional hrs). Babies and young children can be accommodated with special booster seats. Drift, paddle, enjoy the serenity, and, for a touch of drama, keep an eye out for 20-member teams paddling dragon boats.

HEY, KIDS! Travelling the Lachine Canal is like boating up and down a series of steps called locks. Boats are hooked up to the side of the canal, the gates of the lock are closed, and the boat is either lowered or raised, depending on which direction it's travelling. It's pretty cool to watch if you happen to be at a lock when boats are being hooked up, but it can take a while. Boats are also timed to make sure they aren't breaking the speed limit. If they make it to the next lock too fast, they're in big trouble.

LASERDÔME

Montréal has old-world charms, but it also has a futuristic streak. It's hard to spend time here without noticing that the city has a particular fondness for domes. If your kids have visited the Aquadôme (*see #68*), the Biodôme (*see #65*), and the Cosmodôme (*see #57*), they'll probably have big expectations for a place called the Laserdôme. The fact that it's on the bottom floor of a shopping centre is bound to be something of a let down.

They'll get over it, however, once they're strapped into lime-green armor and led into this 8,000-square-foot maze. Lit by black lights, the only evidence of life in this simulated crashed space ship is the green, orange, and purple graffiti that spells out dire warnings. Your family is on an undiscovered planet and you must deactivate the enemy base while protecting yourself and your crew. Suddenly this place seems a lot bigger.

Unlike most lasertag games, which tend to take an every-man-for-himself approach, Laserdôme players are divided into teams. The game, created by Montréal educators, is meant

EATS FOR KIDS For a back-to-the-future experience, head up the street for the ultimate in dome dining. Since the 1940s, **Gibeaus Orange Julep** (7700 blvd. Décarie, 514/738–7486), a drive-in, has been serving delicious orange drinks from a gargantuan sphere, painted like a 100-foot orange. Waitresses zoom around on Rollerblades, serving great fries, hamburgers, hot dogs, roast-beef sandwiches, and even salmon burgers. Don't miss the orange julep, a frothy orange drink that's piped down from the top of the giant orange. If you aren't driving, don't worry, there are plenty of picnic tables.

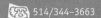

to build communication skills and teamwork. Like most laser-tag games, you lose points for being tagged and have to make your way to a refueling station to continue. At Laserdôme, however, animators lead you through group cheers and strategies and can award points for special teamwork. Once you've finished a half-hour game you complete a debriefing session. This is your team's chance to learn about your strengths and weaknesses. If you want to go back to improve your game, the second game is cheaper, or you can commit upfront to a two-hour block of unlimited play.

Success at this game has little to do with age, gender, or even aim. To win you have to be as good at protecting each other as you are at attacking the enemy. Hopefully your kids will walk away with a few new lessons they can apply not only to laser sports, but to life.

KEEP IN MIND

Reservations a few days in advance are necessary here. If you're looking for something more spur of the moment, check out **Laser Quest** (1226 rue Ste-Catherine Ouest, 514/393–3000). This is a traditional one-on-one, 20-minute laser-tag game in a similar venue.

HEY, KIDS! There's something about having a great name that seems to give you an edge in this game, so you might want to start thinking about an alias before you go. You can choose a favourite character from a movie or book, borrow a name from one of your heroes, or invent your own secret code name. Stay away from really violent names though. In this game, it doesn't help much to be aggressive. It's more important to be smart, use teamwork, and keep things fun.

LITTLE FARM AT ANGRIGNON PARK

Gather eggs, feed the sheep, learn how butter is made, watch a cow being milked, or scamper up a hill to be on level with those height-loving goats. These are all things your child can do for free right across the parking lot from the Métro Angrignon station. Designed by the creative minds from the Montréal Botanical Garden (see #29), this is not your typical petting zoo.

A lovely pond landscaped with tall wild grass and bulrushes introduces toddlers to the swans and geese they may have only seen in books. They can get close enough to have water splashed in their faces from flapping wings. Next they're probably going to want to feed the goats and look up at the llamas on their rocky hill. In a nearby field there are friendly ponies and a cocky burro. Of course there are pigs, sheep, turkeys, chickens, roosters, and all their offspring. Pretty peacocks, pheasants, and emus complete the farm-animal roster.

KEEP IN MIND If you have older kids who tire of farm animals quickly, they'll find plenty to do at nearby Angrignon Park, or at Aquadôme (see #68). The farm closes in the fall but is transformed into a winter wonderland with ice slides and a toboggan hill.

HEY, KIDS! The pigs you'll meet here are a little different from the ones you might find on other farms—they still have their nice curly tails. Pigs are very playful, but often nip and chew on each other. Most farms trim pigs' tails when they're young to avoid infection. On a hot day, you'll find these pigs acting like every other pig by rolling around in the mud. This isn't because they like being dirty, it's because pigs don't sweat like humans, so they have to roll in mud to keep cool.

 3400 blvd. des Trinitaires,
Métro Angrignon

 514/872–4689

 Free

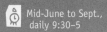 Mid-June to Sept.,
daily 9:30–5

 1–7

Once you're finished with the animal circuit there's a state-of-the-art tractor to climb up on. Don't forget to bring a camera for this perfect photo op.

Educational sessions, guided tours, and farm-related activities are scheduled throughout the day. Children can participate in animal feedings and farm work, or hear talks about the different animals. On some Sundays during July and August there are special events, like a corn roast, or a visit from a bee keeper or apple producer. If you want to stay a while, or entertain a child who turns out to be scared of animals, there's a nice little playground inside the farm. A word to the wise: there's an irresistible hill for toddlers, which can get a little muddy if there's been rain recently. Unless you want to be one of the many parents frantically running after kids, trying to keep them clean, bring a change of clothes and shoes.

EATS FOR KIDS There are plenty of picnic tables here, and it's a very popular spot for impromptu birthday parties. The corn roast is usually at the end of August, and corn is 25¢ a cob. A snack bar at Fort Angrignon (see #51), which shares the complex, opens up at lunch time. Brunch at **Chez Cora** is a great idea (see Aquadôme). **Boccacino's** (7333 Newman, 514/366–0999) has good sandwiches, pasta, pizza, international specialties from chicken teriyaki to grilled lamb chops, and yummy desserts.

MAISON DES CYCLISTS

If you spent an entire summer taking your kids on bike trips in and around Montréal, you'd still have a lot left to explore the next summer, and even the summer after that! In 2001, *Bicycling Magazine* named Montréal the number one major metropolis for biking in North America. That's not surprising when you consider there are roughly 700 km (440 mi) of bike trails in Montréal and its suburbs.

Great. But where to start? With so much available it's worth putting some family time aside just for research. Maison des Cyclists is both the headquarters of Vélo Québec, the bike activists responsible for this extensive bike network, and a pretty café at the intersection of two of the major inner-city bike paths on rue Rachel and rue Christophe Colombe. While nibbling on muffins or a croissant, and watching cyclists speed by, you can peruse maps of the bike trails, rent bikes, or book bike tours. At the very least you should pick up a copy of *Cycling in Montréal*, which contains five nicely detailed maps.

HEY, KIDS! Maybe you've heard of the Tour de France, the most famous and challenging bike race in the world. Well, Montréal has a special bike race just for kids called Tour de l'Île des Enfants. Okay, it's not really a race, but it feels like one. The city shuts down streets (usually the first Sunday of June) so that kids will have a 22-km (14-mi) circuit to bike. You have to be 6–12 to participate, and you have to register. Every year 6,500 kids participate, and the only adults are the tour supervisors. Your parents can cheer for you at the finish line in Jarry Park (*see #43*).

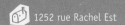

If you're ready to head out, you can take younger kids across the street for a gentle cycle around Lafontaine Park. With its man-made canal and pretty slopes, it's the perfect little trip for kids who are just discovering their balance. Older kids might want to head west along rue Rachel to Mont-Royal Park, though the ride up to the summit is a genuine challenge. If you're not driving, consider calling Taxi-Bike (514/273–6331). A taxi with a bike rack (which will take up to 3 bikes for $3 extra) will take you to the summit. From there you can coast all the way down. Another option is to head east on rue Rachel to the Botanical Garden (*see #29*), the Biodôme (*see #65*), or the Olympic Stadium. Or, head north along rue Christophe Colombe to Île-de-la-Visitation (*see #46*).

EATS FOR KIDS
You can get a full meal at the on-site café, but if you want to head out on a picnic consider **La Boîte à Lunch** (4165 rue St-Hubert, 514/527–2207). In English that means lunch box and they'll pack you a great lunch.

KEEP IN MIND There are some great city-wide bicycle festivals in Montréal when many streets are shut down to allow easy cycling. Tour de L'Île is a family bike tour with 45,000 participants that covers 48 km (30 mi). There's also Un Tour La Nuit, a 20-km (12.5-mi) circuit which allows your family the luxury of biking safely through the streets at night. These usually take place in early June. If you're here for the last week of September you can bike around the downtown core on International Car Free day, when cars are prohibited.

MAISON SAINT-GABRIEL

Take a trip back to Montréal's early years with a visit to this house that re-creates the daily life of some of the city's first women settlers. In the mid-17th century, King Louis XIV offered young female orphans a royal dowry if they would make the long, dangerous trip across the Atlantic to New France where there were nearly 3,000 single male settlers and less than 50 eligible women. The girls who made the trip were known as *les Filles du Roi* (the King's Wards), and were usually city girls who needed to be trained in the skills required of a farm wife in the harsh Canadian climate. Maison Saint-Gabriel is where they were educated by Marguerite Bourgeoys (see #32).

Though the original house burnt down soon after it was built, the second house, with its two-foot-thick stone walls, is still typical of the time. Guides in period costume offer tours of the interior where everything is set out pretty much as it was back then. Pots are ready

EATS FOR KIDS You can picnic here, along the Lachine Canal, or at nearby Wellington Park. Or, head to the neighbourhood institution of **Taverne Magnan** (2602 rue St-Patrick, corner of rue Charlevoix, 514/935-9647). This is classic blue-collar meat-and-potatoes dining. Don't miss the pecan pie.

HEY, KIDS! When you see the King's Wards' beds, you're going to think the girls must have been pretty young, or really short. Though it's true the average person back then was much smaller, there's another reason the beds are so tiny. Because of the cold and darkness, people used to go to bed right after dinner even though they believed sleeping before digesting your food was dangerous. If you notice, there are three pillows on each bed. They used these to prop themselves into a sitting position so they could digest their food while they slept. That's why the beds could be shorter.

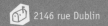 2146 rue Dublin

 $7 adults, $2 children

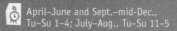 April–June and Sept.–mid-Dec., Tu–Su 1–4; July–Aug., Tu–Su 11–5

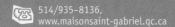 514/935–8136, www.maisonsaint-gabriel.qc.ca

 8 and up

to cook the most popular dish, eel stew; looms are ready to weave hand-spun wool; and the dowry chest given each girl, with its lace and trinkets, sits open upstairs. Check out the grooves that were built into a few of the simple wooden chairs. These were intended for men to rest their arms in while smoking pipes.

If you visit on a Sunday during the summer, the lovely gardens are alive with re-creations of 17th-century feasts and dances that were held to introduce potential husbands and wives. In the winter, kids can imagine the inhabitants huddled around the fireplaces. Believe it or not, Louis' crazy plan worked. Eight-hundred women were sent to Québec between 1663 and 1673, and in six years the population doubled. Close to 20% of Québec's population can trace their roots back to these women.

GETTING THERE The neighbourhood of Pointe St-Charles is definitely off the beaten track for most tourists. It is one of the city's oldest neighbourhoods and still the poorest, despite some gentrification since the rehabilitation of the Lachine Canal. The museum is a short walk from Métro Charlevoix. Just walk down rue Charlevoix, then turn left on rue Wellington until you get to rue Dublin. Or, you can take the Lachine Canal Bike Path and turn south when you get to the St-Gabriel lock.

MARGUERITE BOURGEOYS MUSEUM

Any parent who thinks teachers don't get enough credit will appreciate this museum devoted to Montréal's first teacher, Sister Marguerite Bourgeoys. Kids will enjoy it for two reasons: an eccentric dollhouse exhibit that creates a sense of how remarkable it must have been to be a child settler in New France; and the recently discovered remains of a 2,000-year-old Amerindian settlement in the basement of the adjacent Notre-Dame-de-Bonsecours chapel.

Sister Marguerite Bourgeoys' work in making New France livable for families, and in charming the native children who attended the schoolroom she created out of a stable, has given her status as one of the city's most important founders. Her transformation from privileged teenager to driven New France missionary is quite remarkable. The museum is filled with paintings and information about her life, but it's the dollhouse created by the congregation she founded that's a must-see. Painstakingly crafted during the 1940s, it fills

HEY, KIDS! If you go into Notre-Dame-de-Bonsecours chapel you'll notice chandeliers made out of model ships. For many years this church was known as the Sailors' Church because so many people came here to pray for the safe passage of loved ones making the journey from Europe. If you go outside you'll see bronze statues of angels and the Virgin Mary on top of the spires. When sailors made it over safely, it was a tradition to thank these guardians by donating model ships to the church. Some of the nice ones are what you see hanging.

 400 rue St-Paul Est

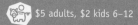 $5 adults, $2 kids 6–12

 514/282-8670

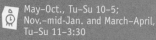 May–Oct., Tu–Su 10–5; Nov.–mid-Jan. and March–April, Tu–Su 11–3:30

 6 and up

an entire room and re-creates 58 scenes from her life with a quirky mixture of detail work and post-war kitsch. Miniature tapestries and gilded furniture are enjoyed by plastic dime-store dolls as Sister Marguerite visits the king of France. Plastic nuns in elaborate black-and-white habits share birch-bark canoes with plastic Hurons and Algonquins; and plastic New France school children learn side-by-side with their plastic Amerindian peers. A somewhat sanitized version of history, no doubt, but it's as charming as it is wacky.

A visit to the lovely Notre-Dame-de-Bonsecour chapel next door is well worth it. The church is one of Montréal's oldest, and the archaeological dig, discovered in 1998 when the church was hoping to expand storage, is both informative and a little creepy. Along with the remains of two early settlements, the bodies of nine nuns who died tending an epidemic are also buried here.

KEEP IN MIND

The visit to the archaeological dig is included in the price, but phone ahead to reserve, since guides don't always seem to be available. Don't leave without climbing the stairs up to the bell tower of the church. The excellent view includes La Ronde (see #10).

EATS FOR KIDS There are many places to eat at Place Jacques Cartier and the nearby Old Port (see #21), but to make this a real journey back to New France, check out **Le Cabaret du Roy** (363 rue de La Commune, 514/902–9000), which re-creates a typical 18th-century restaurant. Everyone is dressed up like settlers ready for a good time. The menu is a mixture of typical New France dishes and some First Nations specialties. There's a kids' menu with drumsticks or sausages. Even if you don't eat here, stop by and visit the dining room. It's great fun.

MCCORD MUSEUM OF CANADIAN HISTORY

Of all the history museums in Montréal, this is the one that feels the most like an adult museum, probably because it was administered by McGill University for many years. There's a fair amount here for kids, however, and since it's right downtown and usually free on Saturday mornings, it's worth stopping by.

Unfortunately the first few rooms in the permanent Simply Montréal exhibit are the least kid-friendly. There are some interesting native artifacts, like a birch-bark canoe, a beautiful cradle board, and wampum beads used as currency, but this period is more engagingly presented at Pointe-à-Callière (see #12), Centre d'Histoire (see #60), and Château Ramezay (see #58). The McCord Museum starts to become interesting in the collection of toys and clothes from upper-class children who lived in the Golden Square Mile. These are dramatized by wonderful floor-to-ceiling photographs of daily life in the early 20th century. The museum has made a special effort to contrast this affluence with the poverty of adjacent

KEEP IN MIND The museum decides annually whether or not admission will be free on Saturday mornings, so call ahead to find out if this is a free year. You can also ask about temporary exhibits, which are often more interesting for kids than the permanent exhibit.

HEY, KIDS! In January of 1998, four days of freezing rain covered the trees of Montréal with three inches of ice. They looked beautiful, but they were really dangerous. The weight of the ice caused tree limbs to come crashing down all over the city, blocking off streets and bringing down phone lines. Power lines and hydro towers were also coated in ice, causing blackouts in many parts of the city for weeks. People were forced to experience part of winter the way early Montrealers did, with no electricity, which meant no heat or light. It was quite an experience!

690 rue Sherbrooke Ouest

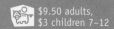 $9.50 adults, $3 children 7–12

 514/398-7100

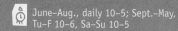 June–Aug., daily 10–5; Sept.–May, Tu–F 10–6, Sa–Su 10–5

7 and up

neighbourhoods like St-Henri and Point St-Charles. Audio equipment provides bilingual readings from Gabrielle Roy's *The Tin Flute*, a seminal French Canadian novel that vividly describes the Dickensian childhood of many French Canadians at the time.

If you're visiting Montréal during the summer, your kids will enjoy the exhibit on Montréal's stunningly awful winters. Observed from a safe, warm distance they seem quite exciting. Even if you're a long-time resident, the old-fashioned sleighs, foot muffs, tiny children's rabbit-fur coats, patent-leather boots, and resourceful old-fashioned winter gear are worth seeing, as are the pictures of kids dwarfed by a five-foot snowfall. There's also a wonderful section on Montréal's worst winter storms, including the 1998 ice storm which blacked out huge sections of the city for weeks. If you're visiting Montréal, make sure you ask a local about this storm. Everyone seems to have his or her favourite survival anecdote.

EATS FOR KIDS Head up rue University, turn right on rue Milton and you'll be at **Amelio's** (201 rue Milton, 514/845–8396). This restaurant has excellent pizza and pasta for unbeatable prices, and a fun student atmosphere. You can also head down avenue McGill College to Place Ville Marie where you can make your way through the fun maze of international delights at **Marché Movenpick** (1 Pl. Ville Marie, 514/861–8181). Kids especially enjoy watching crêpes being made right in front of them.

MONDIAL SAQ FIREWORKS COMPETITION

Since 1985, Montréal has been host to this six-week-long international competition of pyrotechnic art. And art it is. For a full half-hour, two nights a week, rain or shine, the sky is painted with a rainbow of fire. Whatever fireworks show you saw on New Year's Eve 1999, it probably pales in comparison to an average entry.

There are several ways to see the show, each with its advantages and disadvantages. If you're willing to pay top-ticket price, you can watch the action from comfy spectator seats at La Ronde (see #10). Being so close to these powerful explosions is an awesome experience. Plus you get to hear the accompanying music in its amplified glory, which is great if you love movie soundtracks, Pink Floyd, Pavarotti, and Céline Dion. There are risks, though. If the wind isn't in your favor, your child can end up with an eyeful of burning ash. This is more irritating than harmful, but try explaining that to a four-year-old. Also, it's great to see all those fire trucks standing by, but . . . enough said.

GETTING THERE Downtown traffic on fireworks nights is a nightmare. If you're driving, your best option is to see the show from Cité de Havre or from a viewpoint at Mont-Royal (see Olmsted Road). You'll have a better chance of finding a parking spot and beating the westward jams. If you want to see the show from the Jacques-Cartier Bridge, the Métro is a better option. Get off at Métro Papineau. Expect a crowd, but keep in mind that on fireworks nights the Métro is on rush-hour schedule. Don't forget that bikes are prohibited on the Métro on these nights.

La Ronde

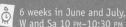 514/397-2000,
www.lemondialsaq.com

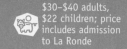 $30–$40 adults,
$22 children; price
includes admission
to La Ronde

 6 weeks in June and July,
W and Sa 10 PM–10:30 PM

 All ages

The other options are free. During the show the city shuts down traffic on the Jacques-Cartier Bridge. Anywhere on or under the bridge is an excellent spot. The crowd is huge but it's well spaced and someone almost always has a radio tuned to the station which broadcasts the music from La Ronde. Unfortunately, there's often someone else who's having a loud, mundane conversation that will suck the splendour from even the best show. You can also try the Old Port (*see #21*), though it's much farther away. Just make sure you walk down to the water so you can see the lower fireworks. Or, try Cité de Havre, just underneath Pont de la Concorde. You'll get a fine ground view and the mood tends to be more respectful. Fortunately, with at least nine shows every summer, you can always keep trying for that perfect night.

EATS FOR KIDS
If you want to go for dessert before the fireworks, consider making a stop at **Frigolin** (1470 rue Cartier, 514/522–4747), near the Jacques-Cartier Bridge. They offer an excellent selection of ice creams and sherbet.

HEY, KIDS! All these countries are competing for the Jupiter trophy. Jupiter was the Roman god of light and sky. He had the ability to hurl thunder at will. Jupiter is also the biggest planet in the sky, more than twice as big as all the other planets combined. When you see the fireworks you'll probably agree that this is a pretty good name for the award.

MONTRÉAL BOTANICAL GARDEN

Kids will have plenty of room to indulge their urge to wander in one of the largest botanical gardens in the world. Second only to London's Kew Gardens, there's a lot more happening here than pretty flowers. There are sublimely-designed landscape gardens; rich, shady forests; and even a re-created First Nations settlement for your kids to explore.

It would take more than a day to walk these gardens from one end to the other, so you'll want to focus on a few areas that are particularly interesting to kids. You could start your visit with the Chlorophyl Room in the Greenhouse. This is a colourful interactive introduction to plantlife designed for school field trips. Unless you have all day, however, or you're visiting in winter, don't waste a lot of time indoors; there's too much great stuff to see outside.

If you've entered from rue Sherbrooke, hop on the free mini-train, which takes you to a stop near the Insectarium (see #44). From here you can walk to the Chinese Garden, the

EATS FOR KIDS The **Casse Croûte du Jardin,** near the greenhouse, is a sunny cafeteria that is open all year. **Le Pavillon Fuji,** next to the Japanese Garden, is only open in the summer. Picnics are only allowed on the benches outside the entrance, near the Insectarium (see #44).

KEEP IN MIND There are endless events and exhibits organized here throughout the year. Typical examples are a Japanese picnic under the flowering crabapple trees in the spring; the Monarch Odyssey, where kids tag monarch butterflies before they head off to Mexico in August; the Magic of Lanterns in the Chinese Garden in the fall; a sugaring-off party in the Tree House in the winter; and the ever popular Butterflies Go Free, in coordination with the Insectarium (see #44). If you're a Montréal resident, your Accès Montréal card gives you free access to the outdoor gardens, so consider planning multiple visits.

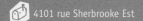
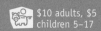

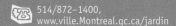
biggest authentic Chinese garden in the world outside of China. Kids will be fascinated by the tiny bonsai elm trees, and they'll love the miniature mountain with its grottos and cliffs. Just make sure you keep a grip on toddlers as there are some steep bits. Next head over to the First Nations Garden. This wonderfully re-created settlement, will give kids a sense of what it's like to live in a northern hunting community. Call ahead, or visit the Web site, to find out when First Nations guides are giving tours in English. If your kids are into fish, walk through the fragrant pine forest to the Japanese Garden where a perfect pebble beach leads up to a pond filled with gold-tinged carp. If you have time, hop the minitrain to the tree house to learn interesting facts about forests, or visit the youth gardens, where local kids maintain their own gardens.

HEY, KIDS! If you visit the First Nations Garden you'll see the frame for a bark teepee. On hunting expeditions, temporary teepees such as this one would shelter two families from one night to several weeks depending on how many moose were around. It could get pretty cold out there, so kids were usually given the task of collecting dry sticks to start a fire. On a really cold night everyone would grease their bodies with bear fat, tie on bear and beaver capes, and huddle together for warmth.

MONTRÉAL PLANETARIUM

With all the different kinds of pollution we have to worry about, it will probably be a while before the world starts really caring about light pollution. With the majesty of the night sky virtually erased, however, just how is the urban kid expected to stay inspired to care about the planet? Fortunately the Montréal Planetarium is so close to downtown that regular trips to this simulated starry night are as easy as they are fun.

A constantly changing schedule of multimedia shows adapted to different ages is another incentive to make repeat visits. A typical show for young kids is *Little Bear's Wonderful Journey,* which explores both the daytime and nighttime sky and acquaints kids with the rudiments of the best-known constellations. There's also a Christmas show that teaches kids about the different planets. More sophisticated shows, like *The Mysteries of Jupiter,* update older kids and parents on the latest, most fascinating discoveries about this giant

HEY, KIDS! Humans have always feared the dark, so it makes sense that we like to have the streets well lit. Using more light than we need, however, has major consequences. Light from most cities is visible 160 km (100 mi) away. This blocks out the stars, destabilizes the environment, and kills many birds and animals that live nearby. It also wastes tons of electricity and money. If we converted to low-voltage lights, used motion-detector lights, and shut off some of the skyscraper lights, we'd have the light we need and be able to see the stars again.

 1000 rue St-Jacques Ouest

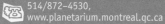 514/872-4530,
www.planetarium.montreal.qc.ca

 $6.50 adults, $2.75
children 5–17

 Daily, show times vary

 5 and up

planet. For really intense stargazers there are more advanced lectures on subjects such as the latest theories on the big bang, or the star of Bethlehem. One of the best shows offered is *Night Sky*. Every evening the night sky is shown just as it would be that very evening if you were seeing it from the countryside. This gives passionate stargazers the chance to study the stars the same way they would if Montréal's skyscrapers weren't blotting them all out.

All of these shows are projected onto the ceiling of the Night Theatre, and watched from reclining seats that encourage dozing. If parenting is starting to burn you out, this may be the perfect outing to do some power napping. With regular visits you may actually find yourself well-enough rested to make it through the entire 45-minute show.

KEEP IN MIND
Each show has an English and a French showing. Call ahead, visit the Web site, or pick up a schedule to find out times. The Planetarium also offers extra lectures, courses, and special stargazing evenings, but these are only in French.

EATS FOR KIDS Head toward downtown and you'll find **Moe's Deli** (1050 rue de la Montagne, 514/931–6637), a spacious, friendly restaurant with big comfy booths. The first floor is pretty much a sports bar, but if you go upstairs you'll find the family dining room. If you want more selection, head to the nearby **Atrium 1000** (*see #67*), where you can browse the comfortable food court and even try a little skating. Through the glass ceiling you'll get a nice view of the real sky.

MONTRÉAL SCIENCE CENTRE

Smack in the middle of the Old Port, one of the liveliest spots in the city, the Montréal Science Centre could be described as a permanent festival of science. Here you'll find hundreds of interactive terminals geared to everyone from preschoolers to postgrads.

Exhibits are organized around themes that change periodically. A typical example of an exhibit for younger children is the Dynamo Lair. Set up like a miniature castle, kids can ponder simple problems like what makes a seesaw go faster when you sit on the end, or how does a bubble machine make square and triangle bubbles. Older kids will get more out of an exhibit like the House Explored, which answers questions about domestic science such as how soap works, or why the leaves in the backyard change colours.

Even in the more sophisticated exhibits you'll find something to entertain younger kids. Terminals don't have to be played with in any order, so there's no need to worry about

EATS FOR KIDS Zoomatic

(see #45) is a great place for a light meal, especially if you sit on the terrace which overlooks the water. **The Food Chain**, just east of the Science Centre, is a food court with just about everything from Italian to Chinese food.

KEEP IN MIND

From the window in the last exposition hall on the second floor you'll get a great view of Habitat '67, a unique building designed by Canadian architect Moishe Safdie. Built at the same time as Expo '67, the idea behind this architectural experiment was to build a high-density urban-housing complex that would still provide families with privacy. From here it looks like a wild, chaotic arrangement of boxes. In reality, these are 158 expensive and sought-after condominiums. Make sure you point it out to kids. It looks like a really fun place to live.

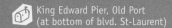 King Edward Pier, Old Port
(at bottom of blvd. St-Laurent)

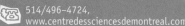 $10 adults, $9 youths
13–17, $7 children 4–12

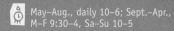 May–Aug., daily 10–6; Sept.–Apr.,
M–F 9:30–4, Sa–Su 10–5

 514/496–4724,
www.centredessciencesdemontreal.com

 4 and up

eyes glazing over. In each exposition hall there are comfy couches where you and a young child can read or play while the rest of the family explores. At an exhibit like Eureka!, kids can get an idea of how much concentration and steadiness it takes to be a surgeon, or they can test the flexibility or density of different kinds of metal. The Science Centre also has an interactive movie theatre that works like a community video game. It's challenging and fun, though seasoned arcade kids will find it a little nerdy.

Budget a good chunk of the day for this trip, and don't even think about visiting every single terminal, especially if you're also planning on visiting the adjacent IMAX theatre (*see #45*). They'll be kicking your family out long before you're finished.

HEY, KIDS! Here's the kind of trivia you might pick up at the Science Centre: The ideal length of time to dunk a dry cookie in a cup of tea is 3.5 seconds. The time it takes for the largest star in our galaxy to emit as much energy as our sun does in one year is 6 seconds. Twenty-five thousand conversations can be carried simultaneously by a single fiber-optic wire. The human sneeze can reach speeds of up to 150 km (94 mi) per hour.

MUSÉE D'ART CONTEMPORAIN DE MONTRÉAL

Surrounded by fountains like some kind of concrete oasis at the eastern edge of downtown, Montréal's most important museum of contemporary art is surprisingly kid-friendly. Host to regular exhibits by international and Canadian artists, it was originally built in the 1960s to showcase Québec's avant-garde painters. Les Automatistes—a Québec movement that emerged in the 40s and 50s—still dominate the permanent collection. This is good news for kids since their credo was radical spontaneity, a principle that is usually close to the heart of many a young *artiste*.

Jean-Paul Riopelle, whose work also hangs in the Museum of Modern Art (MoMA) in New York City, is the most famous of this group. His best-known murals have the same energy as Jackson Pollock's. Thick paint slapped on with a spatula creates work that looks like it has been finger-painted at a preschool for giants. Paul-Émile Borduas was the movement's founder and his rebellious stark blobs of black on white are especially appealing to teenagers. Open the slim drawers with his early sketches and notebooks

HEY, KIDS! Paul-Émile Borduas, father of Les Automatistes, believed that artists should abandon all the traditional rules of art. You know, all the slow stuff, like deciding what to paint, making sketches, and then carefully creating a finished canvas. Instead he believed artists should paint quickly, without thinking, letting their feelings flow out onto the canvas. The goal wasn't to create something beautiful, but to create something honest. If you look at his early drawings in those pull-out drawers, however, you'll see that for someone who didn't believe in sketching, he was pretty good at it.

 185 rue Ste-Catherine Ouest

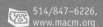 514/847-6226,
www.macm.org

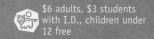 $6 adults, $3 students
with I.D., children under
12 free

Tu and Th–Su 11–6, W 11–9

 7 and up

and you'll find an original copy of the manifesto he wrote and Riopelle signed, *Refus Global* (Global Refusal). Alfred Pellan is another kid-friendly Québec icon. More a surrealist than Automatiste, he created works like *Masquerade* that blend the intensity of Picasso with the whimsy of Matisse. You'll also find playful work from lesser known Québec artists of the 60s. Much of it uses optical illusions and violent colour contrasts. *Twirling Retina* contrasts candy-stripe pink and greens to create a vibrating canvas.

This fun, colourful collection serves as a great introduction to modern art and will probably inspire kids to want to check out the temporary exhibits, workshops, or day camps. Consider dropping by on Wednesday evenings when admission is half price. The scene is more like a gallery opening than a museum and is a great alternative to another family night in front of the TV.

EATS FOR KIDS
La Rotonde, the museum restaurant, has excellent French cuisine. It's pricey, however, and it may be a little swank for some kids. About a 10-minute walk east along rue Ontario, the retro diner **La Paryse** (*see #16*) serves burgers that are modern-day masterpieces.

KEEP IN MIND Don't bother asking for a plan of the museum. There is none, and the friendly staff is weary of answering this question. The floor plan and collection are changed around frequently to accommodate exhibits, so a plan isn't practical. Organized on two levels around a rotunda lobby, this is not a large or complicated museum anyway. Do, however, ask for directions to the difficult-to-find sculpture garden. Henry Moore's *Upright Motive #5* is worth the trouble.

MUSÉE DES MAÎTRES ET ARTISANS

A long with inquisitive minds, most kids have pretty inquisitive hands, which is why arts and crafts are such favorite activities. Sadly, with all the disposable furniture, clothes, and products flooding our world, it seems increasingly rare that these pursuits have any practical value. At this small but beautiful museum, devoted to the ingenuity of Québec craftspeople throughout the centuries, you can bring your children back to a time when craft work was a fundamental part of daily life.

Regular weekend workshops not only give kids an opportunity for hands-on learning, but a context for that learning. The museum is housed in an unusual neo-Gothic 19th-century church, originally Presbyterian until it was bought by the Catholic Church and renovated to suit its more ornate sensibilities. It's the perfect idiosyncratic setting for a permanent collection that will thrill fans of *Antiques Roadshow*. You'll find furniture, textiles, toys, tools, statues, religious objects, and stained glass dating back to the 17th century. There's

EATS FOR KIDS You'll find many family chain restaurants nearby. **Boccacino's** (1790 blvd. Côte Vertu, 514/336–9063) has Italian and California-style food. The more exotic **Ban Lao Thai** (930 blvd. Décarie, 514/747–4805) has refreshing, simple Laotian food along with standard Vietnamese and Thai dishes.

KEEP IN MIND Reservations are a must, especially around Christmas. Though there are workshops all weekend, there's a bonus to coming on Sunday. At 1 PM, lacemakers, weavers, jewelers, and other artisans give demonstrations. If you're fortunate, you might even catch a performance by Fred Pellerin, a kind of Hans Christian Andersen of Québec. Even if Pellerin isn't around, your family can listen to his entertaining stories of village life, learned at his grandmother's knee, on bilingual audio equipment available at the entrance.

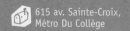 615 av. Sainte-Croix,
Métro Du Collège

 514/747-7367,
www.mmaq.qc.ca

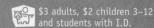 $3 adults, $2 children 3–12
and students with I.D.

 W-Su 12–5

 4 and up

even a bowl once owned by Marguerite Bourgeoys (*see #32*). Temporary exhibits usually focus on one significant craftsperson, or a particular craft, such as lacemaking from Colonial to contemporary times.

Interesting pieces for kids include wooden toys, animals, and a canoe filled with *voyageurs* (*see #50*). Girls may especially like the lacework, and examples of woolmaking. Boys might prefer the section on blacksmiths and iron work. It's the workshops, however, that are the big draw. On Saturday and Sunday, at 1:30 and 3 PM, kids can work on all kinds of simple but fun projects—old-fashioned puppets, Popsicle-stick furniture with interesting carved details, or candy sleds at Christmas. You can do the workshops with your kids, or go explore more adult parts of the collection and the church. Don't hesitate to ask questions—the workshop and museum guides are exceptionally charming and passionate about the work here.

HEY, KIDS! This church looks pretty old, so you might think it's been here a really, really long time. True, it is an old church, but believe it or not it used to be at the opposite end of the city, way, way south on boulevard René-Lévesque. Originally it was a Protestant church, but in the 1930s it was condemned, which meant it was going to be torn down. Instead the Catholic Church bought it for only $1, then took it down brick by brick and reassembled it here like Lego. Not only that, but they did this all in one year!

MUSÉE MARSIL

Amidst the modern bungalows of Montréal's south shore suburb of St-Lambert you'll find a tiny 18th-century brick house, one of the first houses built in the area. This is Museé Marsil, a popular museum devoted to clothes and costumes. The Marsil puts together about three exhibits a year, and uses every wall, alcove, and staircase of the 300-square-foot house for displays. Not only will you and your kids learn fun and interesting facts about the things we wear, you may also pick up a few organizing tips.

Past exhibits have included *Two Centuries of Fashion and Footwear*, from the Bata Shoe Museum in Toronto; *Dressed for the Opera: Costumes from the Opéra de Montréal*; and *Needle to the North: Inuit Coats of Eider*. A very popular show was *The Hippie Generation*. Special care was taken to find original outfits from this era, giving teens something to compare to the currently hip reproductions they might find at the local mall. An interesting theme was the confusion of gender these clothes created. Was that fabulous purple tie-dye djellaba

HEY, KIDS! Do you ever think about the history of the clothes you wear? For instance, nobody knows when the first T-shirt was worn. We do know that the oldest printed T-shirt on record was part of a political campaign in 1948 for New York Governor Thomas Dewey. It was emblazoned with the slogan "Dew-It with Dewey." Now we take printed T-shirts for granted. Can you imagine a future when people might look at our T-shirts in a museum and think that wearing clothes that advertise everything from movies to sneakers is kind of weird?

349 rue Riverside, St-Lambert

 $3 adults, $1.50 children 5–16

 Tu–F 10–5, Sa–Su 11–5

450/923–6601

5 and up

worn by a man or a woman? Imagine the questions caused by the red-shag outfit once worn by Raoul Duguay, a popular Québec poet. The same confusion applied to the collection of original jewelry that included headbands, thick leather and metal rings, and of course the requisite peace symbols. It's probably safe to assume, however, that the Sergeant Pepper silver embroidered-military jacket, worn with skin-tight velour striped pants, was the favourite ensemble of some local male musician.

Although that exhibit had an obvious appeal to older kids, simpler exhibits, like one entirely devoted to hats, are particularly fun for younger kids. This is a charming place to visit all year around, but keep it in mind for October, when you may be looking for some inspiration for Halloween.

KEEP IN MIND
The Marsil has family work-shops every Saturday and Sunday at 2 PM. These are included in the price of admission. Kids might draw their own hippie, or make a hat. In December kids can take advantage of the museum's materials to make their own Christmas stocking.

EATS FOR KIDS Along nearby boulevard Taschereau you'll find all kinds of chain restaurants. For an interesting change, try **Le Commensal** (4817 blvd. Taschereau, 450/676–1749). This is a high-quality, tasty vegetarian buffet with everything from excellent lasagna to interesting variations on traditional meat pies. Food is priced by the pound, which means you pay whatever your plate weighs. It's a good idea to point out to kids that salad weighs a lot less than fudge brownies, and that they should balance their meal accordingly.

NOTRE-DAME BASILICA

Built in 1829, this church is smaller than its Parisian prototype, but it's still a pretty good stand in. In one of the Gothic twin towers stands a 12-ton bell that required a dozen bell ringers to get it going before electricity. Had Quasimodo lived in Old Montréal, he would have had a lot of friends.

Kids who've seen Disney's *Hunchback of Notre Dame* may be disappointed by the absence of gargoyles here, but most will be delighted by the explosion of colour that greets them upon entering. There's nothing cold or ominous about this church. The ceiling of the basilica is covered in gold stars on a night sky background. Music from an organ with 7,000 pipes drifts down from the balcony. On sunny days, three stained-glass rose windows and deep green, red, blue, and gold moldings create a kaleidoscope effect.

The window in the southwest corner of the church might seem a standard scene from the Stations of the Cross, but if you look closely you'll notice that what first looks like

EATS FOR KIDS It's easy to find just about any kind of food you want if you walk east along rue Notre-Dame. If you want a Parisian theme, check out **Claude Postel** (75 rue Notre-Dame Ouest, 514/844–8750). The French pastries are divine, and they offer inexpensive light meals.

HEY, KIDS! Just because there aren't gargoyles here, like the ones you find in Notre Dame de Paris, doesn't mean there aren't interesting sculptures. In 1978, someone deliberately set fire to the Chapelle Sacré-Cœur, destroying it. Fortunately it was rebuilt a few years later. Check out the modern bronze sculpture over the altar. It depicts the stages of life from birth to death. At 16 metres (40 feet) high, it's one of the biggest bronze sculptures in the world. It was brought over from London, England, in 32 pieces and put together like a puzzle.

110 rue Notre-Dame Ouest

 $3

 Daily 7 AM–8 PM

 514/842-2925

7 and up

sand is actually snow. This is Paul de Chomedey carrying the cross up to the top of Mont-Royal (*see #20* Olmsted Road). These vivid stained-glass windows narrate early scenes from Montréal's religious history. In the southwest window, you'll see Jacques Cartier meeting natives as he arrives in what was then Hochelaga. In other windows you'll find Marguerite Bourgeoys (*see #32*) surrounded by native and New France school children, and Marguerite d'Youville, Canada's first saint, surrounded by the poor.

Twenty-minute guided tours are given every half hour and guides are used to being quizzed extensively. If you don't take the tour, don't forget to visit Chapelle Sacré-Cœur, accessible by a passageway in the southeast corner of the basilica. Up to five weddings per day are performed here on summer weekends, so there's a pretty good chance you'll see one.

KEEP IN MIND Mark Twain once said that you couldn't throw a brick in Montréal without hitting a stained-glass window, and true enough the city has a lot of churches. Among the most kid-friendly are: Notre-Dame-de-Bon-Secours Chapel, annexed to the Marguerite Bourgeoys Museum (*see #32*), which has model boats as chandeliers; Église de la Visitation (*see #46*), the oldest church in the city; and if your kids are impressed by Notre Dame they'll be blown away by Saint Joseph's Oratory (*see #8*).

OLD MONTRÉAL GHOST TRAIL

Old Montréal has excellent, child-friendly museums you can visit during the day, but you get a somewhat idealized vision of New France. Come back at dusk, and your child can learn a little about the colony's dark side while having a great time bumping into some of its lively, tragic, and entertaining ghosts. During the summer there are two ghost tours families can sign up for on the spot down at the Old Port: The New France Ghost Hunt on Friday nights, and the Traditional Ghost Walk on Wednesday and Sunday nights. Just look for the booth with the gravestones and skeletons.

Of the two, the New France Ghost Hunt is the most fun. Groups are organized into competing teams and given clues so they can hunt for some of Montréal's founding historical figures, and some of its lesser known victims. These ghosts can be pretty charismatic. Kids might find themselves entertained by a randy, hard-drinking *voyageur* (*see #50*) who jumps out of his skin every time he hears a cell phone or sees a plane. They

HEY, KIDS! Hôtel de Ville, Montréal's city hall, was originally a prison. The green space in the north east corner is where early Montrealers used to hold public hangings. You'll find out more if you meet up with the ghost of Aldolfus Dewey. His was the most well attended execution in the history of Montréal. At your average execution, however, the crowd was usually made up of mostly women and children. Believe it or not, child experts thought this was the best way to teach kids not to be bad. It's a good thing society has changed a lot.

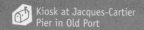
Kiosk at Jacques-Cartier Pier in Old Port

514/863-0303, www.phvm.qc.ca

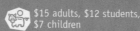
$15 adults, $12 students, $7 children

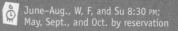
June–Aug., W, F, and Su 8:30 PM; May, Sept., and Oct. by reservation

7 and up

might meet Marie-Hélène Besnard, a *Fille du Roi* (*see #33*) who died of scurvy and bitterly recounts how quickly her husband remarried. Other ghosts include Adolfus Dewey, a notorious murderer who chopped off his wife's head, and Annette Picard who was convicted of sorcery. Kids will also meet more upstanding historical figures like Jacques Cartier, who discovered Canada. Never underestimate the power of morbid anecdotes, however, to get kids interested in history.

The Traditional Ghost Walk will be of interest to older kids, although they'll probably also prefer the Ghost Hunt. A charming, funny guide leads you through some of Montréal's famous sites and relates interesting and sometimes creepy stories. Since you only encounter one ghost, however, younger kids will probably become impatient.

KEEP IN MIND If your kids enjoy this, consider trying the Montréal Historical Crimes Hunt. You must use a map and your deduction skills to meet criminals and their victims. These are held on Thursday and Saturday evenings at the same place.

EATS FOR KIDS If you want to turn this into a total New France experience you might want to try **Le Cabaret du Roy** (*see #32*). There are also plenty of yummy food stalls along the Old Port, and rue de la Commune. **Frites Alors** (143 rue de la Commune) has great Belgian fries and European hot dogs. **Moozoo** (133 rue de la Commune) has yummy sherbets and fresh-fruit treats. Or, you can grab some pizza, a grilled sandwich, or salad at the food court at the **Jacques Cartier Pavilion** right near the Ghost Trail kiosk.

OLD PORT OF MONTRÉAL

Picturesque and always bustling, the Old Port district has so much going on for kids it will take you a good week to exhaust the possibilities.

King-Edward Pier, at the bottom of boulevard St-Laurent, is the halfway point of this mile-long waterfront promenade. You can't miss it if you look for the giant red molecule outside the Montréal Science Centre (*see #27*). If you have young children, walk east over the pretty pedestrian bridges to Bonsecours Island. Here, your kids can test their navigation skills on the Bonsecours basin either in rented pedal boats, or using miniature remote-control sailboats. In the winter the basin freezes over to form one of the best ice-skating rinks in the city. Head further east to climb the beautiful Clock Tower, then take a break while your kids explore the cute little ship-shaped playground next door. The tower is also the place to go if you want to take one of the many afternoon or evening cruises available, or if you have older kids who want to try jet boating, rodeo speedboating, or rock climbing.

HEY, KIDS!
The Science Centre is built on a huge concrete pier that rests on wooden pilings that are a century old. Bet you didn't know that wood doesn't rot as long as it remains underwater!

KEEP IN MIND The magnitude of activities available here can be overwhelming so it's worth browsing the Web site beforehand, especially because activities, festivals, and exhibits change every year. You might also consider taking a *ballade*, a mini-train-shuttle tour of the area (near Jacques Cartier Pavilion). If you're planning on making a day and evening of it, especially with very young kids, you may want to consider buying a family passport ($18) that gives a family of four all-day access to the ballade. If you've got picnic gear, or anything else you don't want to carry around, lockers are available for $2 a day at the Montréal Science Centre.

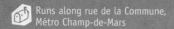

Runs along rue de la Commune,
Métro Champ-de-Mars

514/496–PORT or 800/971–PORT,
www.oldportofmontreal.com

Free

Daily 24 hrs

All ages

A little west of King-Edward Pier, older kids may want to rent electric scooters at **Zap Vieux Port** (Alexandra entrance), or in-line skates at **Ca Roule** (27 rue de la Commune). You can also rent quadricycles, which hold up to four people, near the Jacques Cartier Pavilion. Since these are slightly faster than riding around in a shopping cart, however, you might want to put your money towards something a little more practical. It's worth renting a bike (available at Ca Roule) to explore Parc d'Écluse, with its wacky floral sculptures, or Cité-de-Havre, a pretty island picnic spot. In the winter you can do this on cross-country skis.

Save some energy for the evening when the buildings close to the port are beautifully lit, and the ghosts come out as tour guides (*see #22*). Fire eaters, acrobats, jugglers, and musicians abound, and, of course, this is a prime spot to watch the fireworks (*see #30*).

EATS FOR KIDS There are masses of fast-food outlets down here. For great fries and hot dogs try **Frites Alors!** at the Food Chain, a food court in the same pavilion as the Montréal Science Centre. The food court at Jacques Cartier Pavilion is also quite good and there's a great outdoor terrace which often has good bands in the evening. Or, head over to Cité-de-Havre for a late picnic dinner if you're planning on watching the fireworks (*see #30*).

OLMSTED ROAD IN PARC DU MONT-ROYAL

No Montrealer ever refers to Parc du Mont-Royal by its formal name. This extinct volcano, long considered the city's heart and soul is known simply as the Mountain. Olmsted Road, a gently graded trail which winds around the park for 6.5 km (4 mi), was named after the park's original designer, Frederick Law Olmsted, who also designed New York City's Central Park. This road is perfect for long family strolls.

Olmsted Road has two loops. The lower loop can be accessed by three downtown entrances—on avenue du Parc, rue Peel, and Côtes-des-Neiges—and takes you to the main lookout chalet with its excellent view of downtown Montréal, and then around Beaver Lake (*see #66*). The higher loop will bring your family close to the famous landmark cross that is lit up at night, as well as two other lookout points over north and east Montréal. Cars are prohibited, so expect to pass hundreds of dogs being walked and police patrolling on horseback.

HEY, KIDS! According to legend, Montréal's founder, Paul de Chomedey de Maisonneuve, planted a wooden cross here in 1642. The one you see now, which is almost 30 metres (100 feet) high and lights up at night, was put up in 1924. In August of 1992, to honour Montréal's 350th birthday, 12,000 kids filled a time capsule with messages and drawings about their vision of Montréal in 2142. That's when the capsule will be opened, on Montréal's 500th birthday. If you visit the cross, look for a plaque that shows you where the capsule is. What do you think Montréal will look like then?

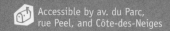 Accessible by av. du Parc, rue Peel, and Côte-des-Neiges

 514/872-2237, www.lemontroyal.com

 Free

 Daily 6 AM–11 PM

 All ages

If you decide to explore some of the wilderness trails that fork off from either of these loops, keep your eyes open for beavers, fox, muskrats, chipmunks, and other wild animals that have made this as much their home as Montrealers have.

It takes a good hour to 90 minutes to complete the lower loop. If you're reasonably fit, and coming from avenue du Parc or rue Peel, take the 250 stairs just north of the Peel access; this will cut off 30 minutes. The higher loop takes about 30 minutes, more if you want to explore some of the alternate trails. Well worth extra time is the Escarpment, a narrower trail that goes along the eastern edge of the mountain and has a stunning view of east Montréal. Keep in mind that the drops are very steep. It's paved well enough for a stroller if you want to keep younger kids safely harnessed.

KEEP IN MIND

If you want to consult a map, or find out more about the history of the mountain or its wildlife, drop by **Maison Smith** (daily 9–5, 514/843–8240), located between Beaver Lake and the lookout chalet.

EATS FOR KIDS You'll find good-quality snack-bar food and ice cream at the lookout chalet. If you want to have brunch before heading out on a hike, **Dusty's** (4510 av. du Parc, 514/276–8525) has been a neighbourhood institution since 1949. Along with one of the best breakfast deals in the city, and Montréal's famous bagels, you'll find great cheese blintzes. Burgers and other deli food are also available if you prefer to eat here after your long hike.

PARC JEAN-DRAPEAU

If all you did one year was head out to this massive park every weekend, you still wouldn't exhaust all the things to do with kids. There are places that are day trips in themselves: La Ronde (*see #10*), the Biosphère (*see #64*), the Stewart Museum (*see #5*), and Plage Île-Notre-Dame (*see #14*). Then there's the lovely, huge park with its three wetland areas, 15 km (10 mi) of bike trails, and all kinds of boating and other fun activities.

The park is really two islands connected by Pont du Cosmos. Look for the geodesic Biosphère and you'll know you're on Île-Ste-Hélène, which is where you'll arrive on the Métro. This is a lovely park for wandering, picnicking, and biking through lush gentle hills and flowery glades. Every Sunday afternoon in summer, from 1 to 8 PM, there's Piknik Elektronik, where a D.J. orchestrates a sort of outdoor rave. Kids love it, and it's a more musical alternative to the Tam-Tams (*see #3*). If you make it as far as the Jacques-Cartier Bridge, check out

EATS FOR KIDS There are snack bars around the park, and Centre Option Plein Air manages a cafeteria. There are so many beautiful picnic spots here, however, it's really a shame to eat inside.

HEY, KIDS! Keep your eye out for some gargantuan public sculptures on Île-Ste-Hélène. You can't miss the fire-engine red *Puerta de la Amistad*. The openings between the three columns play tricks on your eyes, so depending on where you're standing, one opening shrinks, while the other expands. *Man*, by American sculptor Alexander Calder, is 20 metres (58 feet) high and 29 metres (90 feet) wide, making this the biggest sculpture he ever made. *Phare du Cosmos*, a 9.5-metre (30-foot) high robot, used to move. Now he just stands guard, with his eye on Pont de la Concorde.

 South of Montréal via Pont de la Concorde
or Pont Jacques-Cartier

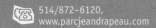 514/872-6120,
www.parcjeandrapeau.com

 Free

 Daily 24 hrs

 All ages

the natural rock face, where kids can take climbing lessons through Centre Option Plein Air
(514/872-0199, www.optionpleinair.com), located on the other side of Pont du Cosmos.

Île-Notre-Dame is the place to head with older, athletic children. This is where you'll find
the Gilles Villeneuve race track, built for the Grand Prix, on which kids can cycle or in-
line skate. You'll also find the Olympic rowing basin where they can boat or watch boat
races in warm weather, and ice skate in the winter. Along with rock climbing, Centre
Option Plein Air manages boat rentals, archery, sailing lessons, day camps, and even
family overnight stays in a hostel. You could play here all day, watch the fireworks at
night, be the first family on the beach in the morning, and be home in time for lunch.
Not bad for a family outing.

KEEP IN MIND There are a dizzying number of concerts, festivals, and special events held here throughout the year. The biggest, most popular family event is Fête des Neiges, which usually runs over the last weekend
of January and the first two weekends of February. Bicycle races on ice, dog-
sled trips, puppet workshops, a 585-square-metre (1,600-square-foot) ice
labyrinth, tube sliding, and ice-sculpting workshops are among the seemingly
endless number of activities. At least 60 zany, costumed characters wander around,
making this the ultimate way to shake off the winter blues.

PARC OMÉGA

18

ack up the gear for a Canadian safari! A journey to Parc Oméga is about a 90-minute drive from Montréal, but it's absolutely worth the time and effort. Driving though this massive 1,500-acre wildlife reserve is the next best thing to setting out on your own expedition into the Canadian North, and, fortunately, quite a bit safer.

Drive along the 10-km (6-mi) trail that winds through valleys, meadows, forests, and lakes and your family is guaranteed to spot moose, bison, wolves, black bears, wild boars, and a splendid variety of deer. Tune your radio to 88.1 FM for an audio guide. Some of these animals are enclosed, but most of them roam free and are not especially shy. Carrots available for sale at the entrance to the park have taught them to anticipate snacks, not trouble, from their human visitors. Expect a friendly welcome from the majestic wapiti, the second biggest species of deer, and expect to run out of carrots long before you run out of

HEY, KIDS! Most of the animals here are indigenous, which means you find them living in the forests of Canada. Some animals, however, have been brought here from other countries. The huge wapiti are from Montana and Wyoming, but they seem to like it here just fine. Keep an eye out for the alpine ibex with their superlong, straight horns. You'll see them prancing easily up and down the rocky hills. They're originally from Europe, but they like the cold weather here and don't seem to have made any dangerous enemies.

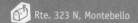 Rte. 323 N, Montebello

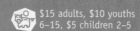 $15 adults, $10 youths 6–15, $5 children 2–5

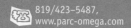 819/423-5487, www.parc-omega.com

 June–Oct., daily 9:30–6; Nov.–May, daily 10–4

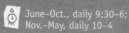 2 and up

opportunities to make other animal friends. To maintain your popularity, buy carrots in bulk before setting out. Bring binoculars for those animals who aren't so willing to get up close. You may want to backtrack, so budget a few hours for the drive through. Budget another hour or so for the hiking trails which allow kids to get a little closer to skittish deer, and to hang out at the newly constructed otter park.

Every season holds the opportunity for different discoveries, but the summer is especially popular because of a thrilling birds of prey show that includes eagles swooping down on rodents and leftover chicken. (This may be a little gruesome for young kids.) Parc Oméga is safe for humans, but be prepared for the small risk that a misplaced hoof may leave a memento on your car's paint job. If this makes you anxious, skip the carrots.

EATS FOR KIDS

The park's restaurant has a panoramic view and a large terrace overlooking a pretty lake teeming with birds and ducks. There are also several picnic sites which are quite popular with the red deer, but don't worry, they won't eat your lunch.

GETTING THERE Take Trans Canada Highway 40 west to Exit 9 for Hawkesbury. Turn right on Tupper Street. Go straight until the stop sign and turn left. Continue until the next light then turn right toward the Long-Sault Bridge. Continue straight and turn left at the next light. Continue straight until you reach Montebello. Make a right on Route 323 north. Parc Oméga is 4 km (2½ mi) down the road on your left.

PEPSI FORUM ENTERTAINMENT CENTRE

In its day, the Montréal Forum was the most victorious home ice in National Hockey League history. For hockey fans, it was a sacred place until the Montréal Canadiens moved to fancier digs at the Bell Centre in 1996. When the Forum was reopened as an entertainment centre in 2001, no one had the heart to entirely gut the much-loved historical landmark. So a small section of wooden stadium seats remain in the lobby along with the big C that was once centre ice.

Hockey pilgrims can watch a free short film of important moments in the Forum's history; it's shown every 40 minutes in the lobby. If your kids are hockey fans, they'll quickly make a beeline for the nearby Canadiens boutique. In recent decades the team hasn't quite maintained its legendary status, but this is still the hockey sweater to own. Fortunately the T-shirts are a cheaper, but equally cool, option.

KEEP IN MIND The Pepsi Forum is still a work in progress, so keep an eye out for new activities and places that pop up each year. Don't waste time looking for the "Parent/Baby lounge" listed in the brochure, however—it doesn't exist.

HEY, KIDS! Legend has it that the Montréal Forum is filled with friendly ghosts who helped Les Canadiens win 23 Stanley Cups. They also helped them win nearly three games for every one they lost at the Forum, from the time it was built in 1924 to when it closed in 1996. Unfortunately with all the movies and video games now here, it doesn't look like the ghosts want to leave. Since Les Canadiens moved to the Bell Centre they've only won about half of their home games.

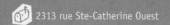 2313 rue Ste-Catherine Ouest

 514/933-6786,
www.legendsoftheforum.com

 Free, some
attractions charge

 Daily 6 AM–1 AM

10 and up

The atmosphere here is still a little cavernous, as the popularity of the entertainment centre has been slow in building. It is, however, developing a reputation as the place to go for the family that likes to explore their separate interests together. In other words, it's a great place to bring teenagers. The AMC movie-plex is renowned for its wide range of blockbuster and independent art films, which makes it possible for parents to catch the top critics' choice while tweens are watching the latest Olson twins.

Upstairs, there's **Legends of the Forum** (514/228-3030), where you can order a drink from the retro lounge while your kids try bowling, play virtual reality games, or follow the latest sports events on 15 different screens. For something more athletic, check out the indoor climbing wall at **Mont-Defi**. This may not be the outing where you form your most cherished family memories, but you are unlikely to argue about what everyone wants to do.

EATS FOR KIDS The obvious place to eat is **Legends of the Forum,** which has all the American classics from burgers to pizza. **Guido & Angelina** (514/228-5225) has surprisingly authentic, affordable Italian food, and the cheesy décor is the next best thing to Caesar's Palace in Vegas. The pastas, pizzas, and meat selections are simple but satisfying. Don't miss the *semifreddo a la nocciola e torrone*, a creamy semifrozen dessert drizzled with chocolate.

LE PETIT ÉCOLE DE JAZZ

The Montréal International Jazz Festival draws an average of one million visitors every summer. Wander around the main site and your family can dance to reggae, pop, salsa, and all kinds of free music with only the merest relationship to jazz. At *Le Petit École de Jazz* (the Little Jazz School) you may find more actual jazz than almost anywhere else. As your child will learn by the end of the 45-minute mock-classroom session, however, *toute peut faire du jazz* (everything can be turned into jazz).

To get the kids warmed up, the team of jazz musicians and singers might start with jazz versions of themes from *The Simpsons* and *Teletubbies*. Then kids from the audience are asked to come up with songs for the musicians and singers to improvise according to whatever style the Jazz Wheel of Fortune stops at. You may hear a calypso version of *Twinkle, Twinkle Little Star*, or a jazz waltz version of the theme from *Sesame Street*. You're also likely to hear a swing version of a Québecois nursery tune or two. This cleverly bilingual show is fast paced enough, though, that a unilingual child won't feel alienated for very long.

EATS FOR KIDS You'll find great food being cooked up all over the Jazz Festival site, from delicious jumbo hot dogs to flowers carved out of mangos. Since the profits from food sales go back into the festival, you may want to support the free shows by keeping your food dollars here. If you're itching to take a break from the crowds, a walk along rue Ontario brings you to **La Paryse** (302 rue Ontario Est, 514/842–2040) where you'll find some of the best and most stylish hamburgers in the city.

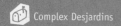 Complex Desjardins

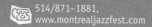 514/871-1881,
www.montrealjazzfest.com

 Free

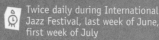 Twice daily during International
Jazz Festival, last week of June,
first week of July

 2 and up

After the show, don't forget to stop by the Musical Playground where kids can slide down a giant saxophone, or march back and forth on the keys of a megapiano. There's free parking for strollers here if you decide you want to wander around the festival site without wheels. Don't let the crowds make you think this is necessary, though; there are always clear pathways roped off in front of the outdoor stages where you can navigate easily between the free shows. It's worth wandering around to check out the different kinds of music—you may be surprised at what your kids end up jiving to.

If you want to attend any of the indoor concerts, a great way to introduce older kids to jazz, try to buy tickets as soon as they go on sale. Visit the web site throughout the year as main events are often announced—and sold out— a good nine months before the actual festival.

GETTING THERE The Métro is the best way to access the Jazz Festival site. To get to Le Petit École de Jazz, bypass the crowds by taking the orange line and getting off at Métro Place d'Armes. There's an underground tunnel that leads directly to the indoor stage. Just follow the signs that say COMPLEX DESJARDINS.

HEY, KIDS! The term jazz was invented in New Orleans. The city had once been under French and even Spanish rule, so there were a lot of different cultures living there, including German and Italian immigrants. Music from the European groups started mixing with the blues, ragtime, and spirituals of African Americans and you ended up with this crazy mixture of beats and styles which became known as jazz.

PLACE D'ARMES

Place d'Armes is so overpowered by the presence of Notre-Dame Basilica, few people, even residents, realize the historical significance of this square. This was Montréal's first battlefield, where a tiny population of settlers fended off regular attacks by Iroquois for decades. If you're down here, it's worth taking some time to help kids imagine Montréal's infancy and to see how much this spot has changed in four centuries.

An unnamed Iroquois warrior sitting at the base of the bronze monument in the centre of the square, and the two other native warriors over the entrance of Canada's first bank—the Bank of Montréal (119 rue St-Jacques)—help set the stage. At the monument, look for a plaque depicting an unarmed Paul de Chomedey de Maisonneuve, Montréal's founder, defeating an armed Iroquois chief in 1644. The settlers of New France did eventually make peace with their Iroquois foes. In 1760, however, the French colony surrendered on this same spot to another enemy: the British.

EATS FOR KIDS Pizzédelic (39 rue Notre-Dame Ouest, 514/286–1200) is a hip, delicious, thin-crust pizzeria with a great kids' menu that includes pasta dishes. Drop by **Claude Postel** (see # Notre-Dame Basilica) to at least see, if not taste, their exquisite pastries and chocolates.

HEY, KIDS! Check out the statue of Sergeant-Major Lambert Closse on one corner of the monument. At his feet is Pilote, Montréal's founding dog. An exceptional guard dog, she is credited with warning de Maisonneuve of an Iroquois ambush in 1644, which could easily have wiped out the earliest settlers. According to a missionary's journal, every morning Pilote oversaw a troop of guard dogs who made the rounds of the area sniffing out potential trouble. When she had puppies, she trained them to do the same. She's more than a small footnote—or pawnote—in history; without Pilote, Montréal might have been a very different place.

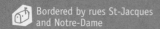 Bordered by rues St-Jacques and Notre-Dame

 Free

 Daily 24 hrs

 514/873–2015

 6 and up

The greatest testament to the affluent British era is the opulent lobby of the Bank of Montréal. Founded in 1817, the bank still has the luxurious marble counters, bronze moldings, and green syenite columns from the days when this was the Wall Street of Canada. In the free museum kids can see a somewhat creepy wax statue of the first teller, cheques written on seal skin, wonderful early piggy banks, and many pictures from those barely imaginable days before computers.

After your visit to the museum, take a closer look at the buildings that surround the east side of the square. The eight-story New York Life Building (505 rue Place d'Armes), built in 1888, was Montréal's first skyscraper. The Aldred building next door (# 507) probably looks familiar. It was completed in 1931, the same year as its much larger twin, the Empire State Building.

KEEP IN MIND Of course the statue, built in the 19th century, tells only one side of the story. If you want a more balanced view take a guided tour of Old Montréal by someone from the First Nations community. The Montréal, Amerindian City Tour will take you to historically relevant sites and tell you about the alliances, trade practices, and conflicts from the other perspective. It will also give you a chance to talk to young native people about their present lives in Montréal. These are available, by reservation, through the nearby Centre d'Histoire de Montréal (see #60).

PLAGE DES ÎLES

Obviously, no city beach will ever yield the same tranquil memories as a beachfront or lakeside cottage. This public beach on Île Notre-Dame, however, is only a 10-minute ride from downtown on the Métro, and is the most well-manicured, pleasantly landscaped beach in the city. Clean, warm water, a large shallow area, no waves, and a small army of lifeguards make this the perfect place to bring young children.

Keep in mind that eating and smoking on the sand are strictly forbidden. The lovely parkland behind the beach, however, is complete with rock gardens, a babbling brook, cascades of daffodils, and picnic tables, all of which make it easy to find a nice spot to picnic. Beyond the water marked off for swimming is an area reserved for pedal boats, kayaks, canoes, and sailboats—all for rent by the hour ($12–$20) at the Water Sports Pavilion. You can also phone ahead and reserve sailing lessons for kids 10 and up through Option Plein Air (*see* Parc Jean-Drapeau). To make your commute easier, you may want to rent chairs and umbrellas once you arrive.

HEY, KIDS! You can't miss the Montréal Casino in the distance. It's that shiny white building surrounded by metal fins that make it look like a giant space ship. When do you think it was built? Last week? Last year? Would you believe it was built in 1967, almost 40 years ago? This was the French Pavilion in Expo '67. The theme of the French exhibit was Tradition and Invention, so they tried to design a building that would look futuristic, and stylish for years to come. We think they did a pretty good job. What do you think?

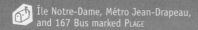

Île Notre-Dame, Métro Jean-Drapeau, and 167 Bus marked PLAGE

514/872-6093,
www.parcjeandrapeau.com

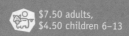
$7.50 adults,
$4.50 children 6–13

June–Aug., daily 10–7

All ages

The problem, of course, is the crowds. You do not want to arrive mid-afternoon on a sweltering July weekend. Plan instead to get here around mid-morning when the beach opens. Anywhere near the little playground on the northeast corner of the beach is a great place to set up camp. You'll get a good hour or two of tranquility before the crowd starts to swell. By then your kids will probably be happy to do some boating or explore the rest of beautiful Parc Jean-Drapeau (see #19).

Another option is to spend the day at the Biosphère (see #64) on Île Ste-Hélène, then hit the beach in the late afternoon, after 4 PM. The admission price is slashed and the anti-litter rules guarantee you won't be arriving at a disaster area.

EATS FOR KIDS
Believe it or not, this beach has one of the prettiest **McDonald's** in the city. There's a large terrace that overlooks the bay. They don't serve breakfast, however, in case you were thinking of coming for an early brunch.

KEEP IN MIND If you're concerned about the water quality at this city beach, don't be. The wetlands on Parc Jean-Drapeau are a source of pride for the scientists at the Biosphère (see #64), the water museum managed by Environment Canada. The park has its own water-purification plant, and while the bays look like they're part of the St. Lawrence, they're actually part of a big man-made lake. The water here is filtered and tested so regularly it's probably safer than most natural lakes.

PLATEAU MONT-ROYAL

Plateau Mont-Royal, a vibrant neighbourhood at the dividing point between Montréal's East and West end, is where one of Montréal's best-known writers, Mordecai Richler, grew up and set his coming-of-age literature. The neighbourhood has changed a great deal since his childhood, but so many young families now live in this charming, lively, and colourful part of town, it'll no doubt pop up again in someone's future memoirs.

Parc Jeanne-Mance at the base of Parc du Mont-Royal (bordered by avenue du Parc) is always packed with kids. There's an excellent playground, a picturesque wading pool, and tons of athletic activities—from baseball to tournament-level soccer. From here you can head out for a stroll along avenue Duluth, a pretty cobblestone street that gives the neighbourhood a village feel. If it's Sunday, head south a bit when you get to boulevard St-Laurent and stop by **Zeke's Gallery** (3955 blvd. St-Laurent, 514/288–2233). The art is always colourful and you may luck out and walk into one of the family-oriented milk-and-cookie art openings held about once every six weeks.

KEEP IN MIND If it's Sunday, head across avenue du Parc for the Tam-Tams *(see #3)* or a stroll along Olmsted Road *(see #20)*. Or hop the 55 Bus up to the Firefighter's Museum *(see #52)*, rue St-Viateur *(see #9)*, Jean Talon Market *(see #42)*, or Jarry Park *(see #43)*, in that order.

HEY, KIDS! On the corner of avenue Duluth and rue St-Denis you'll notice a colourful mural that commemorates the Great Peace of Montréal. This was a treaty signed on August 4, 1701, between France and 39 Amerindian nations. Thirteen-hundred natives came from as far away as New York, Illinois, and James Bay to set up camp here. At the time Montréal only had 1,200 settlers. This peace treaty ended decades of war. It didn't end all the problems by any stretch, but it lasted well into the 19th century. If you go to Old Montréal look for a replica of the treaty in the concrete of Place Royale. The native signatures that look like wild animals are really cool.

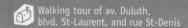 Walking tour of av. Duluth, blvd. St-Laurent, and rue St-Denis

 Free

 Daily 24 hrs

 514/872-2237

 3 and up

If you want to skip Zeke's, keep walking along Duluth and visit **La Grande Ourse** (129 av. Duluth Est, 514/847–1207), where kids can browse handmade wooden toys. With older kids, you may want to walk to rue St-Denis, and head north again until you reach **Valet d'Cœur** (4408 rue St-Denis, 514/499–9970), an eccentric store with games and oddities imported from around the world. Kids of all ages will love the colourful houses just south of avenue Duluth on rue Drolet: colours range from tomato-red and turquoise to apple-green and lavender.

A few blocks further down rue Drolet is Carré St-Louis. This is one of the most beautiful urban squares in North America and you'll often find child-friendly bands playing here for free during the summer. If you still have the energy, continue walking east along rue Cherrier to lovely Parc Lafontaine (*see* Maison des Cyclists).

EATS FOR KIDS The smoked meat at **Schwartz's Deli** is legendary, but if there's a line up, and there almost always is, head across the street to **The Main Deli** (3864 blvd. St-Laurent, 514/843–8126) where the smoked meat is still impressive; only a purist can tell the difference. If you're not a big meat-eating family then you'll love **Café Santropol** (*see* Tam-Tams). Or, head to **Chez José** (173 av. Duluth Est, 514/845–0693) for fresh juices, very healthy milk shakes, empañadas, and sandwiches.

POINTE-À-CALLIÈRE MUSEUM

Make like the earliest settlers and head to the site where Montréal was founded. This exceptional interactive museum is built on what is essentially Montréal's first street corner. Beneath this spot is also evidence of some of the earliest known prehistoric native settlements, the site of New France's first military fort, and its first known cemetery. By seeing how much this small area has changed over the millennia, kids get to learn about archaeology without being overwhelmed with tons of relics.

Kids will learn why the island of Montréal has been such a strategic place for so long. They'll visit the graveyard of the many victims of the war between the settlers and the Iroquois; they'll see the Great Peace treaty signed in 1701 by New France and 39 Indian nations; and they'll love the hieroglyphic-style native signatures inspired by wild animals in the area. As they descend further into the basement they'll be able to look down on six scale models that represent this site as it has been re-invented from a

HEY, KIDS! Before you leave you'll be asked to donate a small artifact of your own. You don't want to donate anything expensive or personal because there's no guarantee it will end up in the exhibit. Can you think of something you have that might show that people from all over the world come to visit this museum? If you took a plane here, maybe a boarding pass. Maybe your parents have matches from a restaurant in your hometown. Maybe your younger brother or sister would be willing to donate the latest happy meal toy. If you don't have anything, don't worry, you can still make a video of yourself saying hi to the people who will be showing up next week.

native village circa 2000 BC to a colony in New France, to the most important industrial hub in British North America, to a 20th-century Canadian city, to this 21st-century ultra-modern museum.

An underground tunnel brings your family to the city's first customs building. On the second floor, artifacts from the once-dominant British culture of the 19th century give way to the invasion of American culture in the 20th century. Through this collection of artifacts from daily life, kids will learn how even an old Barbie can have archaeological value. Before leaving the exhibit, your children will be asked to make a video of themselves, and to contribute a small artifact to the museum's collection. After their visit you may find you have a hard time getting them to throw anything away.

EATS FOR KIDS
There's a museum restaurant with a great view, but it's pricey. **Café St-Paul** (143 rue St-Paul Ouest, 514/844–7225) is a good bet. Or try out the world's best brownies at **Olive & Gourmande** (351 rue St-Paul Ouest, 514/350–1083).

KEEP IN MIND Don't forget to take a trip to the observatory tower at the entrance. It's easy to forget about it, because by the end of the exhibit you end up all the way across the street. This fabulous view of Old Montréal puts the whole exhibit in context. Also there are some can't miss temporary exhibits. In summer 2003, for instance, the museum housed the Dead Sea Scrolls. So don't forget to budget time for that.

REDPATH MUSEUM

This eccentric, charming museum is one of Canada's oldest. In a line drawing of its inaugural ball in 1882, dancing couples seem to swirl dangerously close to the dinosaur skeleton peeking above the ornately carved atrium balcony. It has changed so little over the years you expect to bump into Charles Darwin, or the original Tarzan hiding behind the taxidermied gorilla on the stairwell.

In these days of Jurassic Park and high-tech museums, the Redpath will seem a little dusty to teenagers. Young children, however, adore this place. You'll almost always find preschoolers gleefully scampering up the stairs to check out the 20-foot-tall Albertosaurus skeleton, which takes up a good quarter of the room. A stuffed wolf, coyote, lynx, and various other wild animals pose casually around a pretty annex, as though they were family pets. Gargantuan antlers hang from the still impressive atrium. A small model of prehistoric Alberta gives a sense of what Western Canada

EATS FOR KIDS Head to the east entrance of McGill campus, and then walk east along rue Milton. After a few blocks you'll come to a popular off-campus diner, **Place Milton** (220 rue Milton, 514/285–0011). The breakfasts here are famous, and the prices are very reasonable.

HEY, KIDS! The Albertosaurus you'll find here was a cousin of Tyrannosaurus Rex. This one was actually quite young, about two-thirds the size of an adult. Its name comes from the site where it was discovered in the Badlands of Alberta, one of the richest dinosaur-fossil sites in the world. Over 300 major dinosaur specimens have been found there. Check out the model of what the Badlands might have looked like, back before a major ice age changed its climate from tropical to the northern one we know today.

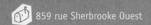
859 rue Sherbrooke Ouest

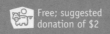
Free; suggested
donation of $2

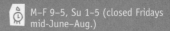
M–F 9–5, Su 1–5 (closed Fridays
mid-June–Aug.)

514/398–4086 Ext. 4092,
www.mcgill.ca/redpath

3–12

looked like back when it was teeming with dinosaurs and had the same climate as the Florida Everglades.

Along with this basic but interesting archaeological exhibit, there's a reasonably large collection of rocks, minerals, and crystals. On the third floor you'll find African Congo masks and an authentic Egyptian mummy. Here you'll find one concession to progress, an interactive computer that shows X-rays of different sections of the mummy. Much of this floor, once devoted to Canadian exhibits, has been moved over to the McCord Museum (*see #31*). Plans for the future include an expanded Ethnology Gallery with antiquities from throughout the world. It looks like the Redpath may be modernizing, but hopefully not too much. If it were possible to have a museum of museums you'd want to place this one inside, like a perfect fossil.

KEEP IN MIND In the fall of 2003, the Redpath started Sunday family workshops. The 2–3 PM workshop is reserved for kids 4–6. The 3:30–4:30 PM workshop is for ages 7–12. Each weekend alternates between French and English and focuses on a different part of the museum, such as volcanoes or primates. The cost is $5 for each child and free for parents. To reserve call Wednesday or Thursday between 11AM and 1:30 PM.

LA RONDE

Built for the Expo '67 World's Fair, this island amusement park has almost too much to do. Give into the "one more ride" plea and you'll be here all weekend. That's not taking into account the shows, special events, and the decision of whether or not you want to go on a fireworks night (*see #30*). Before you go, do a bit of thinking about your family's age, thrill threshold, and priorities and you'll have an excellent time.

La Ronde was purchased by Six Flags in 2001 and has undergone a major makeover, including the renovation of many of the original rides. If you have young, timid, or easily nauseated kids, head to Le Petit La Ronde. After a turn on the miniature roller coaster, bumper cars, or Ferris wheel it should be easy to gauge what your kids are up for. Good family rides in the adult section are the Magic Tea Cups and Le Pitoune (better known in English as the Flume, a modest roller coaster in hollow log boats). Don't miss the super Vulcanizer 3D.

HEY, KIDS! Île Ste-Hélène was once a tiny little island that the explorer Samuel de Champlain named after his wife. Most of it now, including the part that La Ronde sits on, was built out of the dirt excavated to build Montréal's Métro system. So was the entire island of Île Notre-Dame. Montréal needed a lot of land to hold Expo '67, a world's fair that attracted 50 million visitors in the summer of 1967. Instead of taking land away from the city they decided to build these two islands that make up Parc Jean-Drapeau.

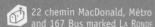

22 chemin MacDonald, Métro Jean-Drapeau, and 167 Bus marked LA RONDE

514/397–2000,
www.laronde.com

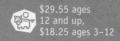

$29.55 ages 12 and up,
$18.25 ages 3–12

Mid-June–Aug., daily 10AM–10:30 PM; May, and Sept.–Oct., hours vary

3 and up

Fixed seats move in a way that simulates a roller-coaster ride through volcanic lava (younger kids can watch it without being strapped into the "moving" seat). The best intermediate rides are the Toboggan Nordique, and the rickety Le Monstre, the world's biggest wooden roller coaster. For intense thrill seekers there are nine rides, including the terrifying Tornado and Vertigo. If you think your children's ambition is a little beyond what they can handle, consider trying Le Manitou, a 24-person pendulum gondola ride. When it gets too much, closing your eyes makes it tolerable.

Of the shows, don't miss "Agora des Hautes Voltiges." Competition-caliber divers dress up as fairy-tale frogs and plunge from the towers of a castle in a kind of diving comedy ballet. They often hose down the audience making this a great way to cool off on a hot afternoon.

EATS FOR KIDS

This is the only Six Flags park where you're allowed to bring your own food. Lockers can be rented near the entrance. You can also leave and return if you want to picnic in Parc Jean-Drapeau (see #19). Otherwise, almost every major chain is here.

KEEP IN MIND You will be practically guaranteed no lines for the rides during the day, if La Ronde is hosting a fireworks competition that night. La Ronde has package deals which include seats for the show, so people wait until evening to get more bang for their buck. Go on a fireworks night, however, and you can wait an average of 45 minutes to get on a ride. If your family has a lot of stamina, consider going on the rides in the morning and returning in the evening for the show. Just remember to get everyone's stamp freshened up before you leave.

RUE ST-VIATEUR

Montréal has plenty of charming streets to stroll with kids, but rue St-Viateur is one of the best for finding delicious food, and diverse people. Once you arrive you may have a hard time leaving—fortunately even the grocery stores have terraces on which to linger.

Though this street is home to many ethnic communities—Greek, East Indian, Italian, Russian, African—the area closest to avenue du Parc is dominated by a large and thriving Hasidic community. About 10,000 strong, it has changed little in the last 50 years. On Saturday you'll find the street teeming with young children dressed in extra formal clothes. Every other day of the week, you're guaranteed to be surrounded by little girls in flouncy dresses and little boys dressed in full black coats and fedoras, whizzing by on bicycles.

You and your kids should definitely visit the legendary St-Viateur Bagel Shop (263 rue St-Viateur Ouest, 514/873–2015). Kids love watching these bagels being made

EATS FOR KIDS Olympico (174 rue St-Viateur Ouest, 514/495-0746) is generally known for having the best coffee around, but keep in mind that they only allow strollers on the terrace. If you're still hungry after bagels, you'll find exceptional souvlaki at **Arahova** (256 rue St-Viateur Ouest, 514/ 274–7828).

HEY, KIDS! The bagel is probably older than either Montréal or New York. A popular theory is that in the mid-17th century an Austrian baker created the bagel to look like a "beugel," the word for stirrup, and awarded it to the King of Poland because he was such a great horseman. In Poland, bagels are a traditional gift offered to new mothers because they are such nutritious and yummy teething rings. Bagels have been around North America for a long time; once cream cheese was invented in 1872, the bagel was definitely here to stay.

 Walking tour of rue St-Viateur, between blvd. St-Laurent and av. du Parc

 Free

 Daily 24 hrs

514/873–2015 for Tourisme Montréal

 All

almost as much as they love eating them. Bagels are sliced from huge rectangular slabs of dough, shaped by hand, boiled in honey water, sprinkled with poppy or sesame seeds, arranged on 5-foot long paddles, and loaded into long wood burning ovens. Along the walls of this stubbornly modest store, you'll find newspaper and magazine articles from around the world debating the long-standing rivalry between Montréal and New York bagels.

Closer to boulevard St-Laurent you'll find an equally thriving community of bohemian families who have also lived in this area for decades. Cafés with lively terraces line the street for people watching. Stop at any one of these when you're ready for a break. Ask the counter person to pour extra frothy milk from a café latte into an espresso cup, sprinkle some chocolate on top and *voilà,* a toddler latte.

KEEP IN MIND This neighbourhood is packed with young families, so it's easy to find places for play or quiet time. The **Mile End Children's Library** (5434 av. du Parc, 514/872–2141) has a good selection of books, a reading area, and a toddler play area. The **YMCA** (5550 av. du Parc, 514/271–9622) has family swims on the weekend that are open to the public. Or head further west along rue St-Viateur until you hit pretty St. Viateur Park, which has a lovely man-made canal and a good playground.

SAINT JOSEPH'S ORATORY

The copper dome of Saint Joseph's Oratory is the second biggest in the world next to St. Peter's Basilica in Rome. It can be seen from many points in the city, but that won't prepare you for your first view of the Oratory from the entrance. The dome's cupola is 200 metres (500 feet) above street level, and a mythical aura is created by the seemingly endless stairs leading up to it (the centre section of stairs is reserved for pilgrims who traditionally climb up on their knees). There's a surprising number of strange and enchanting curiosities for children here.

Near the entrance, kids will be immediately impressed by the magical, though slightly creepy votive chapel. Ten-thousand green, red, and gold candles illuminate walls filled with crutches left here as testimony to the powers of Brother André, the Oratory's founder, who was reputed to have healing powers. His body is kept here in the adjacent tomb, and on the next floor up, his heart is kept in a gold box. Though there are impressive stained-

HEY, KIDS! Brother André worked as a porter at Collège Notre Dame. People started coming to visit him after word spread that he had cured some sick people in the neighbourhood. In 1916 alone he is said to have cured 400 people. So many pilgrims came they had to build this huge church. Long after Brother André died, a man from New York City claimed that a visit to the Oratory cured his cancer. In 1982, Pope John Paul II recognized this miracle and "beatified" Brother André. He needs one more miracle before he's officially made a saint.

glass windows in the lower crypt church, if you don't have all day, head straight to the main terrace for the view. The nearby prayer garden is a serene and pretty stroll through modern sculptures that depict scenes from the Way of the Cross. On the next level up, don't miss a visit to the Oratory Museum, where you'll find a permanent exhibit of nativity scenes exquisitely crafted by artists from all over the world. Over 300 scenes representing 103 countries are on display.

Head upstairs to the sparse but elegant basilica with its 60-metre (150-foot) domed ceiling. Behind the altar is the gorgeous gold- and green-marble Chapel of the Blessed Sacrament. Make sure you have time to visit Brother André's original rustic chapel. A dramatic contrast to the oratory, it's hardly big enough to accommodate more than one family.

EATS FOR KIDS
Le Commensal (3715 chemin Queen Mary, 514/733–9755), across the street, is part of an innovative chain of vegetarian buffets. **Pizzédelic** (5153 Côte-des-Neiges, 514/739–2446), around the corner, is one of the contenders for best pizza in Montréal, and has a children's menu including pasta.

KEEP IN MIND Don't let the number of stairs discourage you from bringing young children who will love the nativity scenes here. The entire site is fully accessible for wheelchairs, and thus strollers. There are even three flights of escalators inside the Oratory. If you visit the prayer garden, try and impress upon kids that this is a quiet place. They'll probably sense this from the atmosphere, and having to whisper can be part of the fun. Don't be mortified if they act up, however. Many visitors don't seem to see the sign requesting quiet.

SIR GEORGE ÉTIENNE CARTIER
NATIONAL HISTORIC SITE

Way out on the eastern edge of Old Montréal, this eccentric house is kept alive with charming interactive plays put on every weekend. The artfully preserved 19th-century house belonged to George Étienne Cartier, Québec's founding father of Canadian Confederation.

Shows change every season, but the concept is the same. Actors dressed in period costume greet visitors as though they are 19th-century guests arriving at the house. Your family might be greeted by a wealthy couple who act as though you've arrived here for a meeting to drum up support for Étienne Cartier's election. Servants who are all too willing to let you in on some of the family secrets may invite you in. Or, a dinner hostess may graciously fill you in on the etiquette of Victorian entertaining. One of the most popular shows re-creates a 19th-century Christmas in an upper-class family home. These charming actors can be shameless hams. The intention, however, is less to give children an accurate history lesson than to give them a feel for life in Montréal around the time of Canada's official birth.

EATS FOR KIDS Head to Place Jacques Cartier (named after Étienne Cartier's grandfather) and you'll find plenty of places to eat. **Jardin Nelson** (*see* Château Ramezay) is a popular choice. If all that formality has you craving something messy, **Arahova** (480 blvd. St-Laurent, 514/282–9717) has excellent souvlaki on pita.

HEY, KIDS! You'll probably notice on the dinner menu that Victorians had very different food than we do. For instance they ate a lot of mutton, something we don't see on our menus very often. Just what is this mutton? In Victorian times it referred to meat from sheep who were more than two years old. It's a lot tougher than lamb, and it has a really strong smell, which is probably why we don't eat it anymore. If you visit India and order mutton, however, you may find yourself eating goat. So ask first, just so you know.

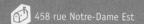 458 rue Notre-Dame Est

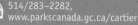 514/283-2282,
www.parkscanada.gc.ca/cartier

 $6.25 adults,
$4.25
children 6-16

April-May and Sept.-mid-Dec.,
W-Su 10-12 and 1-5; June-Aug.,
daily 10-6

 7 and up

The house has the feel of an oversized Victorian doll house. The first room is full of short Muppetlike characters representing the fathers of confederation, and a model railroad that creates a sense of the era. Upstairs there are some interactive computer exhibits that seem a little out of place next to the opulent Victorian sitting room and bedroom. Return downstairs and you'll find a dining room set up for dinner, the kitchen, and the bathroom.

The museum is open during the week, when you'll be given audio headphones in lieu of actors, but it's not the same. The interactive theatre is engaging, while these disembodied voices are kind of creepy, and the equipment is often faulty. It's better to keep this outing for the weekend, when it can be combined with a family stroll through Old Montréal.

KEEP IN MIND Just east of the museum, on rue Berri, you'll see a small building with floor-to-ceiling windows. Walk over and you'll be looking down onto the gymnasium of École Nationale de Cirque, the college that trains many of the entertainers in Cirque du Soleil. It's not open to the public, but recently students have been giving end-of-year shows in Parc Jean-Drapeau, usually in the first week of June. These are a great, cheap alternative to Cirque du Soleil. If your kids are interested in touring a circus school try École de Cirque de Verdun (*see #56*).

SONS ET BRIOCHES

6

Sons et Brioches, loosely translated, means Sound and Pastry, which is exactly what you'll find at this very popular family concert series. Eight times a year, for 30 years, Place des Arts, Montréal's premier performance hall, has been serving up croissants, Danishes, muffins, juice, and coffee before informal hour-long Sunday-morning concerts.

Pastries are served, starting at 10:20 AM, in the beautiful windowed lobby of Salle Wilfred-Pelletier, which overlooks the central outdoor fountains in Place des Arts. Concerts are performed in the Piano nobile, an open performance space just upstairs from the lobby. The audience sits on stairs, a carpeted floor, and some comfy armchairs (if you get there early enough to snag one). Food is forbidden in the performance area, so be prepared to get there a good 30 minutes before the concert starts if you want to eat and get a decent seat.

Concerts usually involve a few musicians, singers, and occasionally some actors. Any theatre is usually in French, so unless your children are bilingual, consider the appeal of

KEEP IN MIND Pick up a Place des Arts program to see if there might be something appropriate for older kids or teenagers. Performances may include concerts by the Montréal Symphony Orchestra and touring Broadway shows. At Christmastime, Les Grands Ballet Canadiens de Montréal does a popular, though extremely expensive, performance of *The Nutcracker* that will set you back about $100 a ticket. In summer 2003, Les Grands debuted a witty, highly original, and entertaining production of *Cinderella*, perfect for teenagers. It's likely to be performed again in the next few years, so keep an eye out for it!

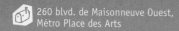 260 blvd. de Maisonneuve Ouest,
Métro Place des Arts

 514/842-2112,
www.pda.qc.ca

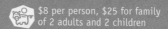 $8 per person, $25 for family
of 2 adults and 2 children

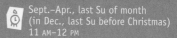 Sept.–Apr., last Su of month
(in Dec., last Su before Christmas)
11 AM–12 PM

 5 and up

the music the main priority. A typical concert might involve a quartet of musicians dueling like musketeers, or some might include operetta or some upbeat jazz classics. The most popular concert is the December concert, which is always the Sunday before Christmas. This is the only concert you will need to reserve for. For all others you can pick up your tickets the morning of the performance. Normally these concerts will be way over the head of any child under 5. You will, however, find many young children here, so don't worry if you want to risk bringing a baby or preschooler along. You'll be shushed if she starts acting up, but there's plenty of carpeted, luxurious play space in the lobby to escape to. For a concert more appropriate for young children, wait until the summer for Le Petit École de Jazz *(see #16).*

EATS FOR KIDS
You're only allowed one pastry per person, which probably won't fill anyone up. For a light brunch, **Café Van Houtte** (260 blvd. de Maisonneuve Ouest, 514/ 849–9923), in the underground passageway between the performance hall and Métro Place Des Arts, has a good selection.

HEY, KIDS! You've probably heard of Mozart, one of the most important composers of all time. Did you know he could play the piano like a pro by the age of three? Or that by four he was writing his own music? By six he'd written his own concert! As a child performer he toured all around Europe, and as a teenager he wrote his first opera. He was never as popular with audiences as an adult, and he had a very hard time making money. Still, in his later years he wrote important music that is still performed today, all over the world.

STEWART MUSEUM

It's hard to believe there was a time when Montréal had to defend itself from invasion by the United States. But that's the reason for this fort, built on Île Ste- Hélène, just after the United States unsuccessfully invaded Canada in the War of 1812.

These days, the fort serves as a re-creation of a Colonial town in New France. In the summer you'll find a baker, a blacksmith, and a carpenter living side by side with the militia. You'll also find numerous Montréal high-school students dressed up in period costume and acting out parts which might involve imprisonment in stocks, or firing off one of the many authentic 18th-century canons. There are guided tours in the morning, but the afternoon is the best time to arrive to see impressive precision military drills. Evening is fun too if you want to try a guided tour by lantern and bump into the occasional ghost. In the winter, kids can take guided tours in snowshoes, learn how to survive in the forest, or learn the sport of curling with authentic 19th-century gear made from cannonballs.

EATS FOR KIDS During the summer there's a Colonial snack bar with typical foods from the time, including meat pies and grilled sausages that bear an uncanny resemblance to contemporary grilled hot dogs. There's also plenty of picnic space in surrounding Parc Jean-Drapeau (see #19).

HEY, KIDS! The Colonial town you'll find here is supposed to have existed around 1758. In reality, the fort was built in 1820, just after the War of 1812. There were a lot of complicated reasons why the U.S. invaded Canada, but the main reason they lost was that their men were unhappy about fighting. Like many U.S. citizens at the time, the soldiers felt that the militia had been created to protect the United States against attack, not to invade other countries. No matter how strong an army might be, if the people aren't solidly behind a war, it's hard to win.

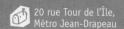

Inside what used to be the ammunitions storehouse is a museum full of old-fashioned weaponry, rapiers, bayonets, muskets, and military costumes from the 18th and 19th century, as well as kitchen and household items. There's also a great scale model of Old Montréal that fills an entire room and is part of a short multimedia show that plunges the room into darkness and spotlights different buildings.

Every year the museum houses temporary exhibits that are often interesting to kids. One exhibit included more than 2,800 lead toy soldiers. Another, which held a bit more interest for girls, was a traveling exhibit on Napoleon's wife, the Empress Josephine, which included royal jewels, gilded swan chairs, and an ermine-lined cape embroidered with silver.

KEEP IN MIND The Stewart Museum offers a unique day camp for kids 9–13. During the month of July, kids get to live in the fort, join the militia, dress up in uniforms, handle antique weapons, experience a sailor's life, and meet natives. Each session includes five days and one overnight stay in a tent and is given in either English or French. Activities change from week to week, so if your child really likes this, he can return for a second week. When he gets older, maybe he can turn this into a great summer job.

STUDIO AT THE MONTRÉAL MUSEUM OF FINE ARTS

4

You can always find something in major metropolitan art museums to interest kids, but the truth is most kids are wired to make art, not look at it. StudiO is the perfect answer to this challenge. Located in a space designed by Frank Gehry, this is an interactive gallery just for kids. Here they can fool around with art all day, any day, for free; and they get to do so in a space that makes their experiments feel as important as any other piece of art in Montréal's most prestigious art museum.

Young children can build colourful foam-brick sculptures as tall as they are, and showcase them in special cubbyholes on under lit panel floors. They can build murals out of an infinite number of fridge magnets, or they can try to recreate famous renaissance still lifes by dressing up in red velvet and lace. Older kids can learn the rudiments of art history or composition by role playing as buyers or gallery owners. They can sketch busts on always available sketch

KEEP IN MIND The permanent collection in the museum is always free. It's huge, so don't plan to see it all in one day. In the first room, look for Salvador Dali's chess set, which has thumbs for pawns and fingers for the remaining pieces. In general, however, the permanent exhibit at the Musée d'Art Contemporain (*see #26*) is more kid-friendly than this one. If you want to visit a temporary exhibit here, there is an admission fee but Wednesday evening between 5:30 and 9 is half price.

pads, or they can don safety goggles and gloves, and hack away at a piece of granite or wood. Kids of all ages will have fun with the many computers set up to experiment with colour composition and self portraiture. All of these things can be done with or without the help of guides, depending on how self-motivated your child is. On Sunday afternoons there are also free workshops built around the exhibits. Just ask for a pass from a StudiO guide.

After your kids have been given the chance to experiment and learn at their own pace they'll probably be more ready to explore the rest of the museum. If you've been playing with them, hopefully, you'll all be equipped with the lingo to discuss otherwise lofty principles like tension vs. harmony, or the differences between narrative and landscape painting.

HEY, KIDS! If you have access to a computer, visit StudiO on the MMFA's Web site and you can play two interactive-art games: *Genre* and *Composition*. Both games will teach you about different kinds of painting styles that you might want to try in your own masterpieces.

EATS FOR KIDS At the museum cafeteria try and get a table overlooking the stairs. These weird stairs are so big that even adults are forced to take either two steps for each stair, or really, really big steps. This makes everyone look like awkward children, something that never fails to delight kids. If you're looking for that classic contemporary kid's meal of burger and fries, head to **Hard Rock Café** (1458 rue Crescent, 514/987–1420).

TAM-TAMS AT PARC JEANNE-MANCE

If you've ever felt you missed out on not being a parent during the Summer of Love, here's your chance to relive something similar for an afternoon. What started as a small African drum circle in Parc Jeanne-Mance in the late 1970s has grown into a massive regular Sunday afternoon drum jam that has been known to draw 4,000 people on especially sunny days.

From noon until sunset, unless it's pouring rain, drummers of all levels, ages, and personalities bang African bongos, plastic milk jugs, elaborate drum sets, and anything else that can make noise, and generally bliss out at the foot of the Sir George Étienne-Cartier statue. An eight-foot-high bronze angel hovers above Étienne-Cartier (*see #7*), who is surrounded by four massive bronze lions and about a hundred amateur and professional drummers. It's probably safe to say this father of Canadian confederation never envisioned himself hosting such a ritual.

EATS FOR KIDS There's plenty of space here for a picnic, but if you want to keep the bohemian vibe going, eccentric and comfy **Café Santropol** (3990 rue St-Urbain, 514/842–3110) has some of the hugest sandwiches in Montréal and a beautiful, shady garden in the back.

HEY, KIDS! The two most popular drums at the Tam-Tams are the *darbouka*, from North Africa, and the *djembé*, from West Africa. They look kind of the same, like very big juice glasses. The darbouka is usually made out of metal or terra cotta, and plastic, goat, or sometimes even fish skin. It has been described as having "the sound of the sea." The djembé is made of wood, and has a low, heavy sound that has been described as "the sound of the jungle." See if you can spot which is which.

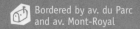 Bordered by av. du Parc
and av. Mont-Royal

 Free

 June–Sept., Su 12 PM–sunset

 514/873–2015
for Tourisme Montréal

All ages

About every half hour there's a pause to suggest that a new "tune" is about to begin. If you've brought your own percussion instrument this is a good time to join in. Once you've been to a few of these gatherings, the charm may start to wear a little thin. Kids of all ages, however, love the event. Toddlers can't help bouncing to the beat, and there are always families dancing in the mall area underneath the statue. Older kids are enraptured by the piercings, tattoos, and, yes, the possibility that there may be illegal substances in the air—although with friendly, casually dressed police patrolling the area, that's not too likely. Just don't spoil the fun by telling them that.

If you're interested in finding out more about drums, or in buying your own, head to **L'Original International** (129 av. Mont-Royal Est, 514/843–1755). The Tunisian owner is an expert in African drums, and he's usually happy to explain the basics.

KEEP IN MIND Here's something for parents who may have missed out on raves. Piknik Electronic is a similar event that takes place on Sunday in Parc Jean-Drapeau *(see #19)*, around Alex Calder's famous *Man* statue. Instead of drums, DJs have set up sound systems with electronic mood music. It costs $5, and is popular with young families.

TRAPEZIUM

With the recent craze in extreme sports it's surprising that trapeze flying hasn't "caught" on yet. Montrealers, however, have been taking up this activity with increasing enthusiasm every year. Courses in trapeze flying are available at École de Cirque de Verdun (*see #56*), but if you want to try one session just for thrills, Trapezium is the place to go.

The trapeze was invented by Jules Léotard, also credited with the invention of the revealing dance wear. Kids may be relieved to find out that leotards are not required to "float through the air with the greatest of ease." Long tights are actually more important since the first position learned is the knee hang. The goal of the first session is to perform a catch. This involves taking off from the platform, hooking your knees, releasing, and then presenting your hands properly to a catcher as you enjoy the ride. Sound terrifying? You'd be surprised how many people take up trapeze flying to help them get over a fear of heights. Instructors are sensitive to people's fears, safety harnesses and nets ensure

HEY, KIDS! Montréal-born sisters Karyne and Sarah Steben are identical twins as well as trapeze artists. They studied gymnastics as kids, and when they were older joined Cirque du Soleil where they performed with, get this, another pair of trapeze artist twins from California named Elsie and Serenity Smith. The Steben sisters have also had regular roles on the HBO series *Carnivàle*, which is set in the circus during the Great Depression. They first appeared on TV at the age of six on a local show called *Satellipopettes*, which was hosted by their father.

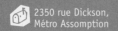 2350 rue Dickson,
Métro Assomption

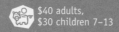 $40 adults,
$30 children 7–13

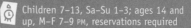 Children 7–13, Sa–Su 1–3; ages 14 and
up, M–F 7–9 PM, reservations required

 514/251-0615,
www.trapezium.qc.ca

 7 and up

that no one gets hurt, and once you get used to the feeling of flying, it's quite a liberating experience.

Eight turns are guaranteed per session, so a session can take anywhere between an hour and two hours, depending on the size of the group (limit is 10 people). Kids 7–13 can only attend the weekend sessions, but kids 14 and up can come any evening as well as weekends. Private sessions are also available by reservation, and lower rates are available for private groups as small as four.

Since Trapezium rents their space from Horizon Roc (*see #47*), you can always do some rock climbing while your children swing. You may, however, find it a little hard to concentrate on climbing if you're also trying to keep an eye on them zipping through the air.

EATS FOR KIDS

Jardin Tiki (*see* Horizon Roc) is always fun. If you're looking for an inexpensive, good Italian meal **Da Giovanni Ancora** (5440 rue Sherbrooke Est, 514/259–3748) is a popular family-style restaurant that's been serving up simple, unpretentious food since 1954.

KEEP IN MIND Trapezium has a reservation system that is something of an exercise in trust. You call and leave a message on their voice mail telling them what session you want to sign up for. If you DON'T hear back from them, consider your reservation confirmed. You can also reserve on their Web site, but make sure you do this at least 48 hours in advance of the session you want. During the summer, Trapezium has been known to set up trial sessions down at the Old Port (*see #21*), though availability is unpredictable. If you're down there it's worth keeping an eye out for them.

WESTMOUNT PARK

This park in one of Canada's oldest and most affluent neighbourhoods is not the biggest in Montréal, but it's certainly one of the most charming. It's easy to imagine earlier days when uniformed nannies strolled perambulators under ancient willows and over the bridges that cross the pretty meandering canal. These days it's a favourite destination for parents and grandparents from all over the city because of an excellent variety of activities for young children.

At the western end of the canal you'll find a tree that looks like it must have been here to greet Westmount's first settlers. Several branches as thick as trunks snake out from a spot just a few feet from the ground. This perfect climbing tree is always crawling with children. Close by you'll find one of the best equipped and poshest playgrounds in the city. Everything is top quality and new, from comfy leather toddler swings to a unique wobbly log that can serve as either a seesaw or

HEY, KIDS!
You can easily walk from Westmount Park to the busiest part of downtown in about half an hour. Can you believe that 100 years ago Westmount was considered so far away that this is where many people had their summer cottages?

KEEP IN MIND Walk one block north along any of the streets that go up from rue Sherbrooke and you'll come to Murray Hill Park, another great place for young kids. Like the name suggests, this park is built on a wonderfully long hill, an ideal spot for gleeful running and tumbling. In the winter it is one of the best tobogganing hills in the city. There's a very good playground here as well, and if you want to go for a stroll through one of Montréal's most exclusive and beautiful neighbourhoods, this is a good starting point.

 rue Sherbrooke at av. Melville

 514/989-5200,
http://westmount.ville.montreal.qc.ca

  Free

Daily 6 AM–12 AM

1–10

balancing beam. In the summer a pretty concrete wading pool in the northeast corner of the park is a popular spot to cool off, and there's always the option of a leisurely stroll along the canal.

Northwest of the playground you'll see a complex of beautiful Victorian buildings. This is the Westmount Public Library(4574 rue Sherbrooke Ouest, 514/989-5300), the first library built in Québec. Even if you're not a member, the children's library is outstanding and a wonderful place for young kids to pass an hour or two. An infant and toddler play area with toys, and comfy places to sit and stretch is the ideal place to browse through the latest titles. Half a dozen computers are set with games appropriate for preschoolers, and several glass cages with hamsters and guinea pigs offer another source of delight for young kids. Just a little west of the library you'll find a fairly large tropical greenhouse. A fun place to hang out in the chillier months.

EATS FOR KIDS Several blocks west of the park, **Java U** (4914 rue Sherbrooke Ouest, 514/482-7077) has great light meals, sandwiches, and fries, and in the summer there's a nice terrace. A little further west, **Toucheh** (351 rue Prince Albert, 514/369-6868) has fresh, inexpensive home cooking and excellent brunches on Saturday, served until 3 PM. It's pretty popular, so reservations on Saturday (it's closed on Sunday) are a good idea.

CLASSIC GAMES

"I SEE SOMETHING YOU DON'T SEE AND IT IS BLUE." Stuck for a way to get your youngsters to settle down in a museum? Sit them down on a bench in the middle of a room and play this vintage favorite. The leader gives just one clue—the color—and everybody guesses away.

"I'M GOING TO THE GROCERY..." The first player begins, "I'm going to the grocery and I'm going to buy... " and finishes the sentence with the name of an object, found in grocery stores, that begins with the letter "A." The second player repeats what the first player has said, and adds the name of another item that starts with "B." The third player repeats everything that has been said so far and adds something that begins with "C" and so on through the alphabet. Anyone who skips or misremembers an item is out (or decide up front that you'll give hints to all who need 'em). You can modify the theme depending on where you're going that day, as "I'm going to X and I'm going to see..."

FAMILY ARK Noah had his ark—here's your chance to build your own. It's easy: Just start naming animals and work your way through the alphabet, from antelope to zebra.

NOT THE GOOFY GAME Have one child name a category. (Some ideas: first names, last names, animals, countries, friends, feelings, foods, hot or cold things, clothing.) Then take turns naming things that fall into that category. You're out if you name something that doesn't belong in the category—or if you can't think of another item to name. When only one person remains, start again. Choose categories depending on where you're going or where you've been—historic topics if you've seen a historic sight, animal topics before or after the zoo, upside-down things if you've been to the circus, and so on. Make the game harder by choosing category items in A-B-C order.

DRUTHERS How do your kids really feel about things? Just ask. "Would you rather eat worms or hamburgers? Hamburgers or candy?" Choose serious and silly topics—and have fun!

BUILD A STORY "Once upon a time there lived..." Finish the sentence and ask the rest of your family, one at a time, to add another sentence or two. Bring a tape recorder along to record the narrative—and you can enjoy your creation again and again.

GOOD TIMES GALORE

WIGGLE & GIGGLE Give your kids a chance to stick out their tongues at you. Start by making a face, then have the next person imitate you and add a gesture of his own—snapping fingers, winking, clapping, sneezing, or the like. The next person mimics the first two and adds a third gesture, and so on.

JUNIOR OPERA During a designated period of time, have your kids sing everything they want to say.

THE QUIET GAME Need a good giggle—or a moment of calm to figure out your route? The driver sets a time limit and everybody must be silent. The last person to make a sound wins.

THE A-LIST

BEST IN TOWN
Montréal Botanical Garden
Biodôme
Centre d'Histoire de Montréal
Jet Boating on the Lachine Canal
Parc Jean-Drapeau

BEST OUTDOORS
Lachine Canal Bike Path

BEST CULTURAL ACTIVITY
Le Petit École de Jazz

BEST MUSEUM
Pointe à Callière Museum of Archaeology

WACKIEST
Fort Angrignon

NEW AND NOTEWORTHY
StudiO at the Montréal Museum of Fine Arts

SOMETHING FOR EVERYONE

ALL AROUND TOWN

MANY THANKS!

T hanks to the many people who helped with this book. To my mother, Katherine Waters, for her enthusiasm, for taking me to London when I was 9, and for letting me explore it with an excellent children's guide book. To my father, David Waters, and my brother Kent Waters for their encouragement and hours babysitting. To Eyal Kattan and Odelia Peer for their flexibility. To Ross Boyd for being my date. To Sarah Musgrave, whose reviews of restaurants saved me countless hours of of legwork. To my editor at Fodor's, Amanda Theunissen, for finding me, and for all her excellent queries. To the other editors I write for whose flexibility and understanding made it possible for me to finish this: Alastair Sutherland, Kim Izzo, and, in particular, Annarosa Sabbadini for her advice. To Annie Charron, Gilles Bengle, and André Bouthillier at Tourisme Montréal. To all the helpful people at the sites listed here for their aid in getting the most out of my visits. To Centre de la Petite Enfance St-Edouard and the Province of Québec for $5 daycare. To Montréal for being such a world class city for kids. And above all, to Ben Waters-Kattan for being the best critic a parent could wish for.

—Juliet Waters

the end